£2.99

WITHDRAWN
from collection

D0477049

HEATHERS & CONIFERS

■ Step by Step to Growing Success ■

David Carr

CROWOOD GARDENING GUIDES

Moulton College
Class No. 635.93362 CAR
Acc. No. T06706
Learning Resources Centre

R
C
✓

First published in 1991 by
The Crowood Press Ltd
Ramsbury, Marlborough
Wiltshire SN8 2HR

© The Crowood Press Ltd 1991

All rights reserved. No part of this publication may be reproduced or
transmitted in any form or by any means, electronic or mechanical, including
photocopy, recording, or any information storage and retrieval system
without permission in writing from the publishers.

British Library Cataloguing in Publication Data

Carr, David *1930–*
    Heather and conifers.
    1. Gardens, heathers   2. Gardens. Conifers
    1. Title
    635.93362

ISBN 1 85223 506 3

Acknowledgements

Line-drawings by Claire Upsdale-Jones.

Colour photographs: Dave Pike for Figs 6, 8, 10, 12, 13, 14, 17, 19, 21, 22, 24,
25, 26, 27, 29, 30, 31, 32, 55, 97, 103, 104, and 110. Natural Image – Bob
Gibbons for Figs 1, 2, 4, 5, 7, 11, 20, 28, 34, 35, 36, 40, 43, 52, 61, 71, 72, 74,
75, 82, 94, 95, 96, 98, 100, 101, 105, 106, 107, 108, 109, 111 and 112; Peter
Wilson for Figs 3, 42 and 102; Robin Fletcher for Figs 33 and 99; and Liz
Gibbons for Fig 38.

Typeset by Avonset, Midsomer Norton, Bath
Printed and bound by Times Publishing Group, Singapore

Contents

Introduction

The reign of popularity enjoyed by heathers and conifers continues unabated with both the gardening public and the trade. The reasons that these trees and shrubs are held in such high esteem are not hard to find. They provide colour and interest from an early age, and often within twelve months or less of planting. Thereafter they reliably provide interest throughout the year. For instance, all but a handful of conifers retain their foliage during winter and so help to overcome the drabness of bare branches and brown earth. Assuming plant selection is made with due regard to prevailing climate, site soil and ultimate size, heathers and conifers are amongst the most labour-saving of plants, needing minimal care and attention. Finally, being versatile, there are varieties suited to semi-formal as well as strictly formal styles of layout.

For the sake of simplicity and convenience 'heather' is used as an umbrella term to include the true heathers (varieties of *Calluna*) and the heaths (varieties of *Erica* and *Daboecia*). In addition to the true heathers and heaths, a number of heather and heath-type relatives are included for discussion in the book — they are ideal companion plants.

HEATHERS, HEATHS AND ALLIES — THE ERICACEA

Heathers embrace an outstanding group of ornamental flowering and foliage evergreen shrubs

Fig I (opposite) This mixed planting of dwarf and large conifers provides an indication of the range of colour and form available.

Fig 2 Daboecia cantabrica (St Dabeoc's heath) – the bold flowers stand out to good effect and they are larger than true heathers.

and shrub-like trees. They vary in size from about 6in(15cm) up to 20ft(6m) or more in height. Typically they have wiry branches. Heathers which grow to 5ft(1.5m) or more are sometimes listed in catalogues as tree heaths.

Characteristically heather flowers are bell-shaped or tubular and carried in clusters or spikes. Shades of pink, rose, purple, wine and white predominate — mostly selfs but occasionally bi-coloured. One exception is *Erica pageana* which has creamy-white flowers. A few varieties have fragrant flowers, and noteworthy in this respect are the sweetly scented *E. arborea* and *E.a.* 'Alpina'.

Fig 3 Erica herbacea *(normally listed as* Erica carnea*) 'Springwood White' – this is probably the best white flowered form around – safe on most soils of average fertility.*

There are very few weeks in the year when some variety or other of heather is not in flower, and from a gardening point of view they fall quite conveniently into two groups according to their flowering season. Winter and spring flowering kinds include *E. carnea*, *E. x darleyensis* and *E. mediterranea* (sometimes listed as *E. hibernica* or *E. erigena*. Winter and spring flowering tree heaths include varieties of *E. arborea*, *E. australis*, *E. canaliculata*, *E. mediterranea* 'Superba' and *E. pageana*. Summer and autumn flowering heathers include varieties of *Calluna* and *Daboecia* plus other *Erica* not listed above.

Foliage Effects

Several varieties have most attractive coloured foliage providing true year-round interest. With these varieties their blooming season is often viewed as a bonus. Foliage colourings come in varying shades of copper, bronze, gold, orange, red, russet, grey-green, pink and yellow. Amongst these so-called foliage heathers expect to find self-coloured, bi-coloured and multi-

coloured varieties, and bear in mind most foliage colourings vary with the changing seasons. Many of the most richly coloured foliage varieties are lime-hating and intolerant of alkaline soils.

Soil Requirements

Following on from the preceding remarks about lime-hating varieties possessing superior foliage colourings heathers in general grow best on acid soils. In fact, with one or two exceptions, summer and autumn flowering kinds are lime-hating and intolerant of alkaline soils. The exceptions are *E. terminalis* and *E. umbellata* which are moderately alkaline tolerant, while *E. vagans* and its varieties will survive when grown on neutral soil. The story is somewhat different in the case of the winter and spring flowering heathers. They are reasonably lime and alkaline tolerant with *E. carnea* being the best choice for alkaline soils.

As a general guide, most heathers are happiest on sandy or light to medium peaty loams which are low in nutrients, particularly nitrogen. On nutrient-rich soils, heathers tend to make

Fig 4 Erica vagans *'Mrs Maxwell' – a close up.*

Fig 5 Erica carnea — *does well on most average soils, flowering from autumn to spring.*

excessive growth, become straggly, weak and die out prematurely.

Heathers vary quite considerably in their soil moisture requirements. For instance, varieties of *E. tetralix* and *E. ciliaris* are moisture loving and thrive on cool, moist, almost boggy, peaty ground. At the other end of the spectrum are those which can adapt to warm, dryish soils. Varieties of *E. cinerea* are noted for their drought-resistant qualities.

Climatic and Site Needs

Heathers, in common with other garden shrubs, show varying degrees of hardiness depending upon variety. Hardiness is the ability of a plant to grow and flourish outdoors, coping with the local climate and standing up to the rigours of the winter weather. The species *Calluna vulgaris*, *E. cinerea* and *E. tetralix* are native British plants.

Fig 6 Calluna vulgaris 'J.H. Hamilton' has *double pink flowers in late summer. Typical of other calluna varieties — an acid soil is essential.*

7

Fig 7   Calluna vulgaris 'Applecross'. This showy, late-flowering scots heather must have acid soil.

They occur naturally on northern moors, mountains and heaths and are the parents of many very hardy varieties. Heathers and tree heaths which originate from areas with somewhat milder climates are reliably hardy in southern and western districts of Britain but they need extra winter and spring protection when grown in cold districts if they are to survive.

Heathers generally flower most freely in open, sunny situations but can adapt to light or partial shade. Varieties grown mainly for their foliage colour are best set out in full sun.

Related Ericaceous Plants

There are literally hundreds of ericaceous plants. Discussed here is but a small selection limited to dwarf or low growing heath-type shrubs well suited for garden use along with heathers. The plants singled out are evergreen with one exception, namely *Menziesia*. They are bushy and/or prostrate and grow between 6in(15cm) and about 4ft(1.2m) in height.

Typical of these ericaceous shrubs are the numerous dainty bell-shaped flowers which are carried during spring and summer, according to variety. The diminutive blooms come mainly in shades of pink, rose, purple and white. The rhododendron included in the collection is the exception – it has yellow and slightly larger blooms than the other plants listed. A few berrying shrubs are also included to extend the nature and range of interest. Their red or black fruits are produced during summer and autumn.

Although a few of the listed shrubs have variegated leaves, do not expect a great deal in the way of bright coloured foliage. The white-margined green leaves of *Pieris japonica* 'Little Heath', for example, are quietly attractive. However, do not underestimate the value of the broad-leaved kinds – they provide a useful contrast of texture when planted alongside the fine needle-like leaves of the heathers.

Cool, light, peaty, acid soils are required, basically similar to the needs of the heathers. One of the major differences is that none of the shrub allies listed are likely to adapt to alkaline soils.

One very useful feature, common to most of the shrubs listed, is the fact that they grow well in cool, partially shaded situations which are less than ideal for sun-loving heathers. So the two groups of plants complement each other well. Although their preference is for partial shade, a few of the shrubs listed do in fact adapt readily to sunny situations provided that the soil conditions are to their liking. Among the sun tolerant are *Arctostaphylos*, *Kalmia* and *Pernettya*.

Most of the shrubs listed are pretty hardy and will survive winter frosts even in cold areas. *Cassiope* is exceptionally hardy, and in severe winters enjoys a blanket of snow.

CONIFERS

Garden conifers have a great deal to offer. One of their many attractions is their versatility. It is normally possible to find a variety of the right size, shape and colour to suit most sites, soils and tastes.

Garden conifers are often lumped together on the basis of size and growth rate. This is the practice at leading garden centres. Taller growing varieties are mostly of upright or erect habit and likely to exceed 10–15ft(3–4.5m) within ten years of planting, being quick or moderately quick growing. Some continue to grow apace, ultimately making very large trees. These are unsuitable for small gardens where they outgrow their space and present a hazard to people and property.

Many dwarf and slow growing conifers are of

bushy or spreading habit. Also included are carpeters and ground-hugging conifers, plus others of upright or erect growth.

Shape and Form

Conifers are noteworthy for the infinite variety of naturally occuring inherited shapes without any need for special training or manipulation. Explore the range fully when garden planning so as to exploit their naturally neat habit and distinctive pleasing outlines to the full. Some of the more usual, natural shapes which will be encountered – weeping, rounded, spreading, conical, shrubby and ground cover – are best illustrated graphically (*See* Fig 9).

The idea of 'training' conifers should not be ruled out. For anyone who has the time, know-how and inclination, the scope is enormous, provided suitable varieties are selected in the first place. A visit to a good topiary garden or well-managed bonsai collection should dispel any lingering doubts about the potential in artificial forms.

Fig 8 Conifers have a great deal to offer by way of contrasting shape and form – as well as foliage colour – as seen in this picturesque setting.

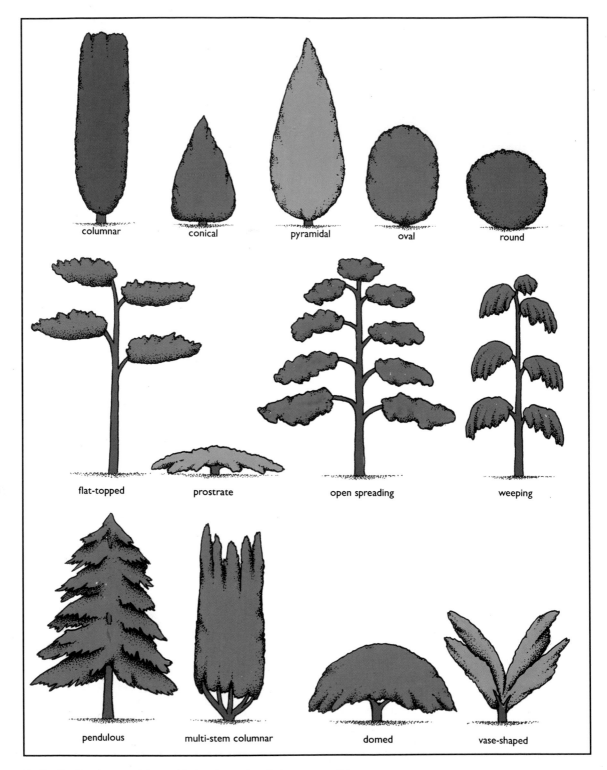

columnar   conical   pyramidal   oval   round

flat-topped   prostrate   open spreading   weeping

pendulous   multi-stem columnar   domed   vase-shaped

Fig 9   Conifer shape and form. All the above descriptive terms will be encountered in catalogues.

Fig 10 Thuja plicata 'Zebrina' is a moderately quick growing tree of conical habit.

Foliage Interest

The foliage of the garden conifers listed is highly ornamental and attractive, more than making up for the obvious lack of flower colour. Depending on variety, the foliage comes in various shades ranging through gold, bronze, copper, blues, greys, greens, browns, reds and variegated silver or gold effects. Some conifers change their colour with the season – this is typical of *Cryptomeria japonica* 'Elegans'. The green or brownish-green summer foliage changes through brown to pink to reddish brown in winter. In addition to colour, much conifer foliage has a pleasingly aromatic quality, with a clean pine scent. This is particularly noticeable in pine (*Pinus*) and spruce (*Picea*) on warm, sunny days. There is also considerable textural variation on offer ranging from the dense, close nature of some of the

junipers to the open, airy growth associated with some monkey puzzles.

Many varieties produce the familiar fir cones popular with children and flower arrangers. Cones are produced when, and only when, the conifer reaches maturity. This may be anything from five to seven years with such as the Korean fir to upwards of twenty to thirty years in the case of cedars. The biggest and most interesting cones are produced by varieties of *Abies* (fir), *Cedrus* (cedar), *Picea* (spruce), and *Pinus* (pine).

Soil Requirements

Conifers vary quite considerably in their needs and tolerances depending on variety. However, most garden conifers grow well on cool, moist, acid-to-neutral loams. Possible exceptions to this generalization are varieties of pine and juniper which seem to manage very well on light sandy

Fig 11 Hybrid larch – foliage and cone detail come out well on this close up.

soils of reasonable fertility. In fact they flourish in much drier and less nutrient-rich soils than most other conifers. *Chamaecyparis*, pine and juniper can adapt to alkaline as well as acid soils and are happy on most 'heather' soils. In the case of pines, the accumulation of fallen needles tends to make the soil increasingly acid to the benefit of many neighbouring ericaceous plants.

Climate and Site

It is a well-established fact that many of the largest conifers are found growing in cool, mild, moist areas with above average rainfall. This provides a good indication of their preferences. However, it does not mean that conifers cannot be grown successfully in the drier, more southerly areas with their warmer summers. Indeed a number of varieties of *Pinus*, *Cedrus*, *Chamaecyparis*, *Cupressus* and *Juniperus* grow and flourish in warm, dryish conditions. In fact many varieties of *Pinus* seem to prefer lower than average rainfall.

When choosing a variety of conifer for a particular site there are sound practical reasons for considering shape and form, apart from aesthetic factors. Flat-topped trees like cedar and some pines are best avoided in areas subject to heavy snowfalls otherwise branch breakages caused by the weight of snow are risked. Multistemmed trees like *Taxus* and *Chamaecyparis* are liable to be forced out of shape by snow and even torrential rains so it is best to grow single-stemmed specimens in areas of high rainfall and heavy snowfalls.

Because of the evergreen nature of conifers and the fact that the foliage has to stand up to winter gales, storms and freezing winds, the likelihood of leaf scorch is greater than with many deciduous trees and shrubs. It is therefore very important not to overlook the question of shelter in exposed gardens.

The matter of sunlight and shade, in relation to conifers, is of particular significance. Some conifers, notably pines, are light demanding and intolerant of shade. Most varieties with blue, silver

Fig 12   The blue spruce (Picea) *looks well when grouped with other conifers – but it needs sun, space and an acid soil.*

or gold foliage colour up best in full sun. Other conifers are less exacting and tolerate, or even prefer, light or partial shade especially when young. This is the case with *Thuja* and *Abies*. Perhaps the most important thing to watch out for is the intense permanent shade cast by dense foliaged varieties such as *Chamaecyparis* and *Thuja*. This can be a serious problem where tall varieties are grown in small gardens. The effect of heavy shade is to wipe out any possibility of underplanting.

In town gardens the likely effects of pollution need to be taken into account when choosing varieties for new plantings. To generalize, evergreen conifers as a whole are less tolerant of town smoke and grime than many deciduous trees and shrubs, and it is therefore vital to select carefully. Varieties of *Taxus*, *Cedrus*, *Chamaecyparis*, *Juniperus* and *Thuja* are amongst the most pollution tolerant. Some of the most sensitive varieties to pollution are *Abies*, *Pseudotsuga*, *Picea* and *Pinus*.

CHAPTER 1

Using Heathers and Conifers

There are several long standing and strong arguments for including heathers and conifers in any garden. Indeed, these plants are considered virtually indispensable from the aesthetic and labour-saving point of view. Conifers, heathers and their allies are mutually compatible with each other, and are also environmentally friendly plants. They do not for instance require continued and heavy applications of artificial fertilizers in order to survive and flourish. In fact, soils that are over-rich in nutrients encourage disease-prone plants with a relatively short life expectancy. When grown in surroundings to their liking, these plants are, to all intents and purposes, ecologically self-maintaining. From a conservation angle, heathers and their allies are amongst the best of bee-attracting plants providing generous supplies of pollen and nectar. Mention should be made too of berrying kinds like *Arctostaphylos* and *Vaccinium* and their contribution to the food supply of birds.

WHERE TO PLANT

In most gardens it is usual to have some form of boundary demarcation. At one end of the scale are physical barriers providing privacy, seclusion and shelter, and at the other are token markers.

Boundary Hedges and Screens

These provide considerable scope for the use of conifers and heathers but when choosing for hedging and screening purposes, think carefully about the end result. The ultimate height of hedge is very important. Some tree heather varieties are unsuitable for training as tall hedges, over say 5ft(1.5m) in height. On the other hand some varieties of conifers are difficult to keep below this height. Leyland cypress *(Chamaecyparis x Cupressocyparis)* and Lawson cypress *(Chamaecyparis lawsoniana)* are typical of the more rampant growers. Consider too the anticipated treatment of the hedge. Is it to be severely clipped, or even topiary trained, or to be free form? Where children and grazing

Fig 13 One or two carefully positioned taller conifers like these Chamaecyparis lawsoniana *varieties will provide privacy for some secluded corner.*

Fig 14   Conifers are highly versatile – suitable for most gardens from the geometric style to the informal setting as shown.

animals are likely to be in direct contact with hedging, avoid poisonous plants like *Juniperus* and *Taxus*, although it should be stressed that the danger to children is minimal. How much of a barrier does the hedge need to be? Conifers like *Chamaecyparis x Cupressocyparis*, *Taxus* and *Thuja* make more resilient physical barriers than tree heathers, but when it comes to visual screens and decorative features tree heathers are hard to beat.

In open-plan housing estates, where there are restrictions on the erection of walls and fences and the planting of hedges, it is often still possible to provide a token division. One attractive way to achieve this end is to plant ground cover, and here, low-growing heathers and prostrate conifers planted alone or with other suitable ground cover plants open up various possibilities. Incidentally, not only can this form of planting serve as a boundary marker, but it can also discourage pedestrian traffic from taking short cuts. For this type of planting to be truly effective, the ground cover beds need to be at least 4ft(1.2m) in width.

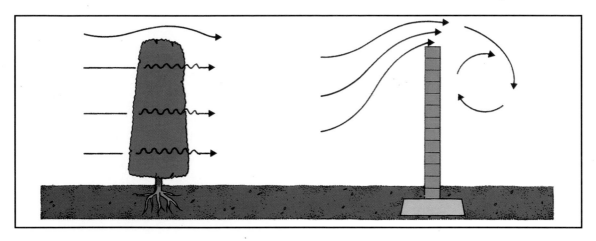

Fig 15 A permeable windscreen such as hedge allows air to filter through and slow down. A solid barrier like a wall results in air turbulance as wind swirls over the top.

Another problem which can arise in the open-plan garden, or elsewhere for that matter, is the lack of privacy from nearby houses. The strategic siting and planting of one or more tree heathers or medium-sized conifers can effectively shield ground floor windows.

Windscreens

A hedge or screen of wind-firm conifers creates a superior type of windscreen. Air speed is effectively filtered and slowed down to the benefit of plants (and occupants) in the garden on the leeward side. Compare this to a solid wall or fence which can result in violent air turbulence within the garden as the wind gusts over the top. Consider heathers and conifers too for shelter within the garden – around sitting areas and to protect other wind-tender plants for example.

For any windscreen to be effective it must be suitably sited. And unless there are extenuating circumstances this is most likely to be across the direction of the prevailing wind. Most screens need a return at one or both ends to prevent wind swirling in behind the screen. Height is also important because it has a direct bearing on the depth of shelter provided. For calculation purposes, given a minimum screen/hedge height of 6ft(1.8m), it is reasonable to assume that a sheltered area equal to about four times the screen/hedge height can be enjoyed.

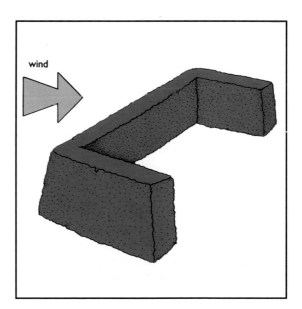

Fig 16 Face the windscreen into the direction of the prevailing wind and provide returns at each end to prevent windswirl on the sheltered side.

Noise Baffle and Dust Shield

All too often in built-up areas, the nuisance of noise and dust are tolerated without question. Rarely is any effort made to improve the quality of life by planting a shrub screen. Tall, dense and preferably fairly thick hedges or screens are effective when it comes to deadening noise from passing traffic, industrial estates, schools, public parks and open spaces. Where dust and litter 'blow' is a problem, substantial hedges act as traps. Dust levels and the unsightliness of litter within the garden are greatly reduced.

Backdrops

Provided they are carefully sited and tastefully selected, tree heathers and tall conifers make excellent backdrops for flower beds and borders. Other garden features also look well positioned against such suitable backgrounds – fountains, statuary, specimen trees and shrubs included.

One useful tip is always to place light-coloured features in front of darker backgrounds. For instance a pink flowered weeping cherry or golden yew are seen to excellent advantage when fronting a backdrop of green conifers.

It is a common practice to combine the role of hedge or screen with that of backdrop.

Edging

As a legacy from earlier times, box and lavender are often used as edgings to beds and borders. Clipped box looks good all year round. It is neat and tidy when well maintained but it does need regular clipping, and for some it lacks the sought-after seasonal variation. Lavender too is popular with its grey-green scented foliage and lavender, blue, purple or white flowers in due season.

It is surprising that heathers have not been more widely used for edging, especially when they have so much to offer. They can be grown on a wider range of soils than either box or lavender, assuming of course that suitable varieties are selected. They provide a much

Fig 17 *Golden conifers, like this* cupressus, *stand out well when seen against a darker background.*

greater choice of foliage colour than either box or lavender, and need less frequent clipping to shape. They have a bonus of flowers, and look equally at home in formal as well as informal settings.

Try heathers as edgings to surround island beds of low-growing shrubs or bedding. Winter and spring flowering dwarf heathers around bedding roses create foliage and flower colour at a time of year when the beds are otherwise drab. In cold, bleak gardens in particular, winter and spring flowering heathers are invaluable as edging to spring bedding, and they offer out of season colour.

Heathers are effective too as front-of-border edging used in conjunction with other shrubs and conifers. A row of dwarf heathers, planted along the top of a retaining wall, will soften any

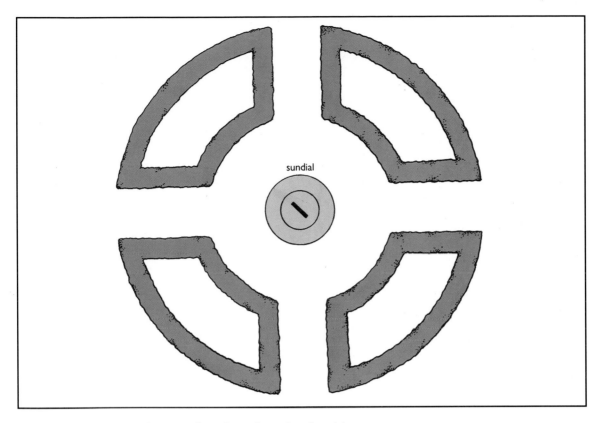

sundial

Fig 18   Dwarf heathers make an excellent alternative to box for edging such as knot garden beds.

tendency towards harsh outlines, and they are similarly suited to planting at the foot of a wall. They can also add informality to the foot of a hedge where they are remarkably tolerant of the competition for food and moisture. Use heather allies to edge north-facing or shaded hedges and walls.

Various dwarf and slow-growing conifers are suitable for edgings although conifers in general tend to be a bit on the expensive side for this type of work.

Ground Cover

By virtue of their low height and bushy or spreading habit, dwarf and intermediate heathers and heather allies are eminently suitable for use as ground cover, and they represent a popular choice. However, the potential that ground-hugging conifers of wide spreading habit have to offer is rarely fully appreciated. These shrubs also provide excellent ground cover and deserve to attract much greater attention. Compact, low-growing conifers too are extremely useful particularly when planted as companions to heathers. Some have very attractive blue colourings, as indeed have some of the spreading varieties. Blue foliage is noticeably absent amongst heathers and so contrasts well. Use spreading and compact low growers with heathers in sunny situations. Many are shade tolerant and dual purpose and you should use these varieties with heather allies in shaded situations.

17

Fig 19 Erica cinerea 'Pink Ice' looks well with blue or grey foliaged conifers.

Fig 20 Arctostaphylos uva-ursi *(bear berry).*
The delicate bell-shaped flowers are followed
by red berries in late summer and autumn –
making this an attractive ground cover plant.

Ground cover lends itself for use in an immense variety of situations. Mention has already been made of its use as boundary markers in open-plan gardens, but perhaps their most familiar role is as rock garden plants, where heathers and their relatives are usually seen in the form of blanket cover broken up with rocks and stones. This type of planting works well and is very suitable on slopes. It is an excellent form of treatment for exposed hillsides where hardy varieties stand up better than most other shrubs to the buffeting of wind. One word of caution: on a level site, low-growing heathers and their dwarf relatives, when unrelieved by taller plants, can look rather uninteresting in a small modern garden setting. On flat sites there is much to be said in favour of drifting heathers in with taller subjects.

Once well established, a heather-conifer type

of complete ground cover requires a lot less maintenance than, for example, grass. In fairness it should be pointed out that ground cover does attract and trap litter. When massed, heathers undoubtedly do attract cats from far and wide. Think twice about massed plantings in areas with a high cat population or be prepared to use repellants constantly or put up with their fouling.

Focal Points and Accent Plants

In some of the remaining large country gardens there is plenty of evidence to confirm that conifers and other evergreens were used extensively to break up large expanses of grass, paving or gravel areas. If suitably scaled down, in size and proportion, these ideas can be emulated in present day gardens.

Tree heathers and erect-growing conifers are well adapted to use singly as specimen focal points in grass and in other open spaces. In addition, there is scope for using them in pairs — one either side of a doorway, steps or entrance — to frame or simply capture attention.

Focal points can become truly eyecatching spectacles when made up of groupings of matching or contrasting tree heathers and conifers. For interplanting amongst low-growing shrubs

Fig 22 The golden cypress (Chamaecyparis) seen here, provides a fine focal point — towering above neighbouring plants.

Fig 21 Thuja 'Rheingold' and golden juniper (Juniperus) make a good focal point.

and border perennials to give extra height, and serve as accent plants, tree heathers and erect-growing conifers are reliable and useful and rank with the best.

Growing in Containers

For hundreds of years, successive generations of conifers have been grown successfully in containers. Perhaps the best known and longest running form of pot culture is bonsai. Many varieties of conifer are eminently suited to this type of work, but the art of bonsai is by no means confined to conifers — nor indeed to evergreens.

Of the conifers listed, varieties of

19

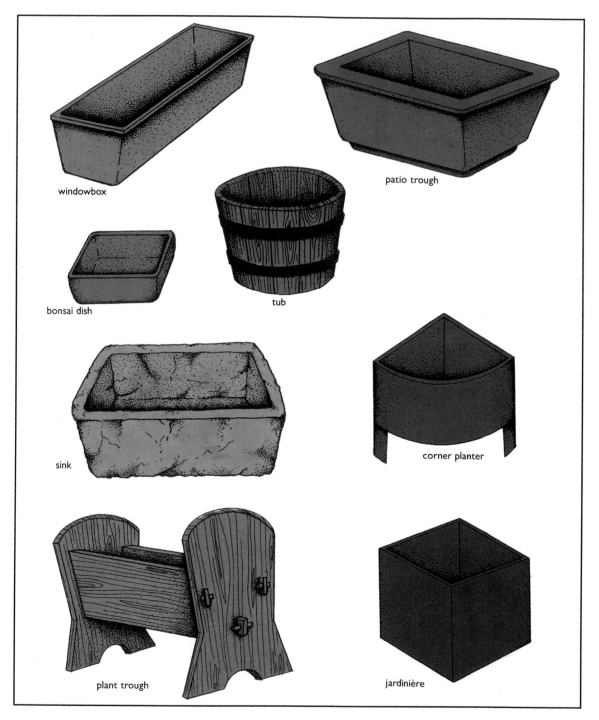

Fig 23 *Heathers and conifers can be displayed to good effect in a wide range of containers.*

Chamaecyparis and *Juniperus* are most at home in containers and do not resent a restricted root run. Some varieties of *Taxus* and dwarf *Pinus* also do well.

Using heathers in tubs and windowboxes is a more recent development. As a general rule, the alkaline-tolerant varieties are easier to manage successfully in containers than the acid-loving kinds. This is no doubt due, in part at least, to the build up of salts and lime in the potting compost, where mains water is used for irrigation purposes.

PLANTING POLICY GUIDELINES

Frequently at the planning stage, insufficient regard is given to the more practical considerations of garden layout and too much emphasis is put on appearances alone. Any one of a number of factors can foul up even the best laid schemes:

1. Will the proposed layout work? Pay special regard to the realistic *needs* of users and not to some hypothetical situation.
2. Does the size and nature of the garden impose any obvious limitations? It is futile, for example, to design on the grand scale when the reality is a modest-sized plot.
3. Can the proposed plans be implemented or are they likely to be thwarted by lack of expertise and know-how? Think of the necessary resources of labour, cash and machinery.
4. What about the availability of plants and materials? Will they be to hand as and when required?
5. Is the calculated timescale to complete the job a realistic one? It invariably takes longer than anticipated. Give this matter very careful thought when attempting sizeable jobs.
6. Have the implications of future maintenance been fully considered? Many a fine layout is ruined by the lack of subsequent maintenance. A little extra forethought at the planning and planting stages should minimize future frustrations and disappointments.

Planned Obsolescence

When starting with an empty bed, border or garden, and plans are for a predominantly conifer layout, think things through. It is going to take standard nursery-sized conifers several years to fill their allotted space and in the interim there are basically two options to consider. Either put up with bare earth or plant up with shorter-term fillers. These may or may not be heathers, but heathers would be coming to the end of their useful life by the time slow-growing conifers reached their ultimate size and so they represent one sound choice. However many opt to infill

Fig 24 This young Cedrus atlantica *will spread to 20ft (6m) or more within 20 years.*

with herbaceous perennials which are selectively thinned out as the permanent plants enlarge. Others prefer to use annual bedding in due season.

Another possibility is to plant up with extra large stock which would give greater immediate, visual impact. But all is not on the credit side – there is always quite a considerable premium to pay for the increased size. As a general rule, standard nursery stock, if of good quality, will grow away and establish more quickly than the larger shrubs and trees.

It is most important to match plant requirements as nearly as possible to the prevailing climate, site and soil. To ignore this rule is to invite trouble. The other cardinal rule is to plant only at the appropriate season, and only when the weather and soil are suitable.

Aesthetic Considerations

There are many angles from which to view what is loosely called style. Style is all about plant choice, positioning, arrangement and the way in which plants are treated. All factors which inevitably influence any garden setting.

One of the most clear cut and distinctive styles is the formal layout in which plants are usually arranged with regular geometric accuracy, symmetry and balance. They are then subsequently trained, clipped and manicured with architectural precision. Topiary work is an obvious manifestation of the formal layout. At the other end of the style spectrum is the asymmetrical, informal, natural layout where plants are allowed to grow and develop in an organized but random fashion.

Heathers and conifers lend themselves to both

Fig 25 A conifer garden with an interesting variety of colour and form is labour saving.

extremes of style as well as to the intermediate, compromising forms of treatment which are generally adopted. It is usually easier to design and plan a formal layout and obtain a satisfactory result than an informal one. The informal garden requires a great deal of know-how and skill if it is not to get out of hand.

Colour

It is never easy to prescribe colour schemes for others, simply because the use of colour is very much a matter of personal preference and individual taste. There are, however, a number of widely accepted guidelines which can help when dealing with colour in the garden.

As a general rule, the most pleasing and successful colour schemes are relatively simple. Those of a busy, multi-coloured nature are always in danger of giving a restless, spotty effect. For this reason it is generally advisable to set out heathers in groups of at least three to six plants of the same variety. It is almost always preferable to have fewer varieties, arranged in larger groupings than to opt for a larger number of varieties with fewer plants of each. This is one of the major problems which the specialist heather and conifer collector has to reconcile when arranging numerous different varieties in a visually pleasing manner. In medium to large-scale plantings, a popular practice is to adopt a patchwork quilt effect of sizeable drifts, broken up with taller shrubs and conifers.

When deciding colour schemes, there are three main options to consider:

1. Use plants of the same variety or colour – recommended in small layouts.
2. Harmonize two or more shades of the same colour. In the case of heathers, pink and rose go well together, as do pinks, mauves and purples.
3. Contrast colours for more eyecatching, startling effects. Gold or yellow foliage heathers, contrasted with bright blue conifers or red flowers are a highly successful combination. Other pleasing colour contrasts include green

Fig 26   The dark green yew (Taxus baccata) *provides an excellent backdrop to red flowers and variegated foliage.*

with pink, red, gold or white; purple with yellow; and pink, mauve or purple with white.

By exploiting the visual impact that different colours have on the viewer, the use of colour to create illusions of size and distance is a practical ploy.

Muted and subdued shades like mauves, greens and browns give an illusion of distance and are best planted furthest away from the main viewing point where they give an impression of depth. Conversely, strong, bright colours such as gold, yellow or red are best planted near to the viewpoint since they give an impression of nearness, and if planted at the boundary, will bring that forward and the garden will seem smaller. Where dwarf plants are involved in the scheme of things, the same rules apply provided the plants are massed and raised. For instance, a raised bed or rockery of purple-mauve heathers will create an illusion of distance in a small garden, when set well away from the viewpoint.

Bright colours make a plant stand out more when compared to a similar sized plant in green, bronze or purple. Hence the good advice of using, for example, a yellow foliaged specimen plant in front of a dark backdrop.

Colours such as red, yellow and deep pink give the impression of warmth. On the other hand blue, green and white create a cool feeling. Use pale colours such as pink cream, white or yellow in shaded dark corners – they stand out much better than deep shades of red, blue or green.

When planting in groups, it is advisable to introduce at least one or two golden varieties to avoid the so-called funereal effect of unrelieved dark green foliage. This advice applies in particular when setting out groups of tall conifers.

Give just as much thought when introducing additional colours to an existing layout as to when starting afresh.

Texture

Heathers – and some conifers – have a sort of light, almost feathery quality to their foliage and they benefit from contrasting with heavier, bold-leaved shrubs. For instance, the coarser textured rhododendrons, azaleas and pieris provide a pleasing contrast to the lighter foliaged *Taxus* and

Fig 28   Ginkgo biloba (maidenhair tree). The distinctive leaves of this deciduous form provide a change of texture in a conifer garden.

Fig 29   The feathery foliage of this Cryptomeria japonica *turns coppery or purplish brown in late autumn.*

Fig 27   Pines (Pinus) *have very distinctive long, needle-shaped leaves, providing an interesting textural contrast with other conifers.*

Juniperus. In an average small to medium-sized garden, it is good policy to reserve bold-leaved shrubs for the middle to back of border positions.

Occasional clipping of heathers and conifers results in a closer, more dense type of foliage.

Shape and Size

The implications of size, timescale and space requirements are discussed on pages 21–2. In addition, when designing any layout, there are a number of other guidelines which need to be kept in mind from an aesthetic point of view. The natural shape and growth habit of any shrub or tree will have an important bearing on its garden use.

Tall, narrow varieties are generally well suited to confined spaces, as hedging or screening, as backdrops, as well as for accent plants in beds and borders. They also lend themselves to framing views, doorways and entrances. On a smaller scale, narrow, erect plants are extremely useful in raised beds, sink and trough gardens.

Weeping, upright-spreading and rounded conifers are admirable as single-specimen focal points. They also look well in group plantings with tall, narrow varieties, and when reflected in water.

Conifers of unusual shape and form – natural or manipulated – often become a talking point when set out to relieve a flat surfaced area. This may simply be due to the interplay of sunlight and shade or to shadow effects during early morning

Fig 30 *Weeping conifers, like this cypress* (Chamaecyparis) *make good individual specimens.*

Fig 31 *Blue spruce* (Picea) *makes a pleasing specimen in a sunny spot as seen here.*

Fig 32 The narrow golden yew (Taxus) provides a stark contrast to the spreading juniper (Juniperus) in the foreground.

or late evening. Whatever the reason, they will add interest to an otherwise flat and uninspiring surface.

USING HEATHERS AND CONIFERS

Incidental Planting

In small, established, well-stocked gardens, there is usually only limited opportunity for setting out heathers and conifers, and planting is frequently phased over several years as existing plants are replaced.

Heathers, set out in small groups to provide a welcome splash of colour, make a good starting point for many. Winter flowering and/or foliage varieties, both of which give a long season of colour, are eminently suitable for the purpose especially in the smaller garden. Other varieties, which give a shorter but glorious burst of bloom, may be more suited to larger gardens where the initial need may be to plug a seasonal gap of interest.

Fig 33 Lane's golden cypress (Chamaecyparis) – a large golden, pyramidal tree normally grown as a specimen. Is a good tree for mixed groupings in large gardens.

A small selection of the possibilities which heathers and conifers alone – or in conjunction with other plants – have to offer the garden designer now follows. Do not be put off by terms such as heather garden and heath garden, and the theoretical differences between such rigid classifications. Be familiar with the terminology but aware that in practice these uncompromisingly defined schemes rarely happen. Individual tastes usually decree that the rigid needs adaptation.

Heather Garden

The heather enthusiast may wish to plant up or extend a collection of flowering and foliage heathers to the exclusion of all other plants.

26

Provided site and soil are right and the plants are set out in groups, the effect can be quite restful. Bank or slope plantings, emulating a hillside scene, are popular, as are terraced scapes. In many instances, flat beds and borders are the order of the day and need not disappoint. Set taller varieties to the back of borders and in the centre of beds, fronting off or surrounding with dwarf kinds.

The selection of varieties is usually on the basis of site suitability, flower and foliage colour, and season of interest. Many gardeners opt for year-round colour but others prefer to concentrate on a particular time of year.

The Informal Heath Garden

A heath garden is a progression on from the purist heather garden and is suited to much the same type of settings. A variety of plants are normally included in the layout and heathers, conifers and dwarf brooms like *Cytisus* and *Genistas* are in keeping, with maybe an odd tree or two – *Betula* is popular especially when underplanted with rhododendrons, camellias or pieris.

The Peat Bed or Garden

In districts where the soil is alkaline and unsuitable for lime-hating plants, the construction of a peat bed or garden used to be the answer. Planting was then carried out on the lines of a heather or mixed heath bed. Unfortunately, today, costs have risen to prohibitive levels and anything other than a miniature peat bed is ruled out on the grounds of economics alone.

A Garden for All Seasons

Year-round colour is a practical proposition assuming flowering as well as foliage heather and conifers are used.

Where the aim is to provide year-round flower colour, it is important to understand the consequences of so doing. It means that although

Fig 34 Vaccinium vitis idaea – *summer and autumn berries prolong the season of interest.*

there is flower colour at most times of year, the quantity of flower at any given season is less impressive and less concentrated than would have been the case if flowering was confined to two or three bursts of bloom. This is where coloured evergreen foliage scores, providing as it does a backbone of year-round interest, so allowing the emphasis to be put on spasmodic yet brilliant displays of bloom.

The idea of augmenting heather and conifer colour with companion plants has considerable appeal. Spring flowering bulbs, summer flowering shrubs and autumn berrying kinds open up many possibilities.

The Seasonal Garden

It is stressed that if gardeners opt for a riot of flower colour at some chosen season, and to forfeit bloom at other times, it is vital to include a few foliage varieties and attractive conifers to give out-of-season interest.

Planting in Containers

Container growing opens up many and varied opportunities but it is important to understand

27

Fig 35 Cryptomeria japonica *'Pygmaea'* – grown for it's seasonal changes in foliage colour. It dislikes dry conditions.

Fig 36 Chamaecyparis pisifera *'Parslorii'* A compact mound former which is particularly useful for sink gardens.

that before embarking on such an enterprise, provision for year-round watering is a must.

Tubs, troughs, sinks and windowboxes enable conifers and heathers to be grown on patios, paved courtyards and terraces provided there is a reasonable level of sunlight. Sink gardens, incorporating one or two dwarf conifers, and alpines, never fail to provide a talking point. Winter flowering heathers, with dwarf conifers, make a pleasing winter and spring windowbox alternative to such as pansies, bellis and polyanthus.

The Pygmy Pinetum

The idea of a bed, border or entire garden devoted exclusively to conifers has a certain appeal, and is an excellent way to accommodate and display a collection of dwarf and slow-growing varieties. If possible, some effort should be made to create changes of levels to give a more natural effect. Stepping stones set amongst the conifers allow the plants to be tended and enjoyed to maximum advantage.

A pygmy pinetum is a labour-saving feature which can be incorporated into virtually any size of garden. There are varieties suited to both sun and partial shade.

One possible drawback of such permanent plantings is the need to use temporary fillers which subsequently need to be selectively thinned. This is never a popular pastime but even this difficulty can be overcome to a large extent by plunge planting in a bed. The plants are set out, complete with pots, and plunged up to their rims in soil, or peat, to conceal the containers and provide a moist, cool root run. The pots must have their drainage holes covered with gauze to exclude the entry of worms and other soil pests. One of the great advantages of plunging plants is that they can then be lifted and rearranged, or spaced out, without harm.

The Shaded Garden

In lightly shaded gardens it is still possible to create an interesting feature using conifers of

Fig 37 Pygmy pinetum. Stepping stones make for ease of access, improved viewing and convenience in tending plants.

varying textures, in the company of heather allies, to provide both flower and berry colour. In these situations dwarf rhododendrons and bulbs, dwarf conifers and heather allies, all make effective underplantings for trees such as *Betula*.

Topiary and Foliage Gardens

Conifers can be clipped and shaped into various architectural forms in a formal or whimsical style. Boxes, globes, corkscrews and animals are but a few of the possibilities. *Taxus* is one of the best and easiest conifers to handle. Topiary features are popularly displayed bordered by gravel. Another idea worthy of consideration is to use the lawn.

To extend the range of ideas, consider clipped heathers, along with other evergreens like box,

Fig 38 Juniperus chinensis 'Variegata' – the variegated foliage of this juniper appeals to the connoisseur.

29

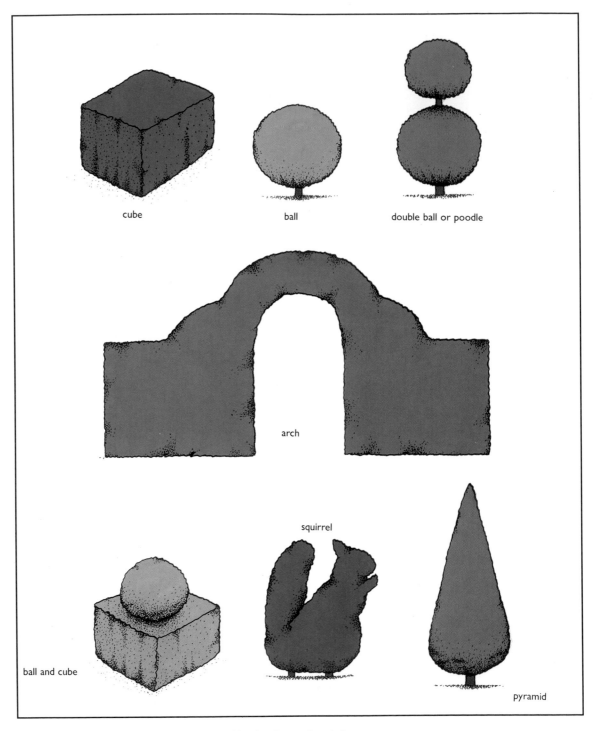

cube

ball

double ball or poodle

arch

squirrel

ball and cube

pyramid

Fig 39 Topiary opens up countless opportunities for the garden designer.

Fig 40 Juniperus horizontalis *'Douglasii'.*
Worth seeking out for its blue foliage.

to edge bedding plants to make a parterre or knot garden. A flowerbed edged and subdivided into compartments, using dwarf evergreens, is frequently referred to as a parterre. It differs from a knot garden which is made up of a number of individual edged beds subdivided by paths.

CHECKLIST – DESIGN IDEAS

No matter whether there is a new garden in the making, or improvements are being made to an existing one, the first stage is to draw up a list. Include all the features which spring to mind as desirable for the new or revised layout. This should ensure that opportunities are neither missed nor forgotten although rarely is it possible or practical to include all the initial ideas. However, a list can help in the decision-making process by pin-pointing the best ideas to retain. The less important ones can then be discarded.

A full site assessment is necessary to establish which features can be incorporated and which are impractical.

1. *Style and Colour* Decide on the type of layout (formal or informal) as well as colour, season and nature of interest required.
2. *Hedging, Edging and Screening* Weigh up the need for as well as the nature, height and purpose of these features. Is a physical barrier needed? What about hiding eyesores? Consider privacy, wind protection, noise and dust. Is a backdrop desirable?
3. *Incidental Use* It may not be feasible to plant up heathers and conifers in quantity – consider the scope for patch or dot planting.
4. *Ground Cover and Underplanting* Do not ignore the benefits of low maintenance, and weed-smother value of dwarf heathers and prostrate conifers for ground cover and under-planting.
5. *Beds and Borders* When thinking about traditional beds and borders do not overlook other ideas such as raised beds, peat beds and plunge beds.
6. *Containers* Planting in containers can add greatly to the interest of a patio, balcony and courtyard area. Containers can also provide a practical solution for the housing of plant collections. Window and wall boxes, tubs, troughs, sinks and planters all make for pleasing effects when sensitively treated.
7. *Special Features* A rock garden, a conifer or foliage feature, a shade, water or wall garden, a parterre or knot garden can all add character and interest to any garden. Mixed plantings, incorporating other than heathers and conifers will add to the range of flower colour, texture and foliage interest.
8. *Specimen and Accent Plants* Think seriously about using tree heathers and conifers as specimens to create a focal point, as dot plants to give height and interest in beds and borders, or to frame views, entrances and doorways.

CHAPTER 2

Autumn Scene

There is plenty to see and enjoy during autumn in an established garden, well stocked with heathers and conifers. The late summer and autumn flowering varieties of *Calluna*, *Daboecia* and *Erica* are in full bloom while in favoured beds and borders, expect the earliest of the winter flowering heathers to begin to show flower colour by late autumn. In addition, there should be plenty of foliage interest among conifers, foliage heathers and their allies. There is still much to do even though the days are growing shorter and growth is slowing down and the first frosts of autumn are nigh.

AUTUMN CALENDAR

A simple routine repair and maintenance programme is all that is necessary in a well-stocked garden where improvements are not being considered or implemented. This maintenance routine is not particularly demanding work, but it does require a modicum of attention to detail and obviously has to be adapted to suit individual circumstances. This is a good time to catch up on any outstanding jobs and get the garden into good shape for winter.

Initial Clean Up

Hoe and hand-weed beds, borders and ground cover areas. Be meticulous around the bases of tree heathers and conifers. Give special attention to newly planted ground cover. It is vital to prevent persistent weeds getting a hold amongst ground cover — aim to get them out by their roots with minimum disturbance to plants.

Failure to do so is to build up trouble for the future. A fern trowel is an effective tool for the purpose and the job is best tackled when the soil is moist. Clean out hedge bottoms, forking out the biggest weeds and raking out litter — this destroys breeding grounds and overwintering refuge for pests and disease organisms, and is important at any time but essential with evergreens. Otherwise risk bare stems where the basal foliage is deprived of light due to weed growth.

Edging Grassed Areas

Where specimen conifers and heathers are planted in grass, always maintain an appreciable collar of bare earth around the base for at least the first few years after setting out. This not only reduces the competition for nutrients and moisture by the grass roots but also prevents grass growing up amongst the basal foliage in the early days. Clip grass edges and, where broken, neaten off with a spade or edging iron, cutting down vertically against a straight-edged plank of wood.

Leaf Removal

Do not allow falling leaves to blanket cover heathers or conifers — the risk is defoliation. Pick over or rake off falling leaves regularly during autumn. Then, when the last of the leaves are down, have one last gathering up before winter.

Disposal of Leaves

Deciduous leaves from trees like birch and beech can be made into leaf mould — a valuable organic material suitable for mulching or digging in. Alternatively leaves can be added to the general compost heap. Composting should be limited to deciduous leaves as evergreen leaves are highly resistant to rotting and do not make good compost.

Grubbing Out

Take a close look around the garden looking for any dead, dying or sickly plants. This is of special significance where a new garden has recently been taken over. Carefully dig out and remove all casualties. If left, they could become a source of infection for healthy plants. Diseases like heather wilt and various conifer rots for example, can be kept in check by the prompt removal of affected plants. Where plants have died out because of disease, remove infected soil in the immediate vicinity of the roots and then disinfect in and around the resulting hole before replanting.

In the case of mature gardens where plants are nearing the end of their useful life, think carefully about their fate. Is it feasible, for instance, to propagate from them before grubbing out?

Where there is evidence of chronic overcrowding amongst long lived conifers (and they obviously need more space to develop if permanent damage is not to be done) set about selective grubbing out immediately.

In time some mature conifers can become a potential hazard to property. This situation normally arises where tall conifers are growing too close to dwellings or other structures. Be concerned where the distance between tree trunk and building is less than tree height. At this distance mature tree roots can damage building foundations. Damage can all too easily arise either directly, by roots forcing their way among the foundations and breaking them up, or indirectly through differential soil heave or settlement. Differential settlement is normally worst on heavy clay soils which expand and contract to a greater extent when subjected to alternate wetting and drying than any other soil. The problem created by trees alongside buildings is mainly because of the fact that large trees take up copious amounts of water, and the soil is dried out and contracts in the region of their root run. In turn this causes uneven settlement of the soil

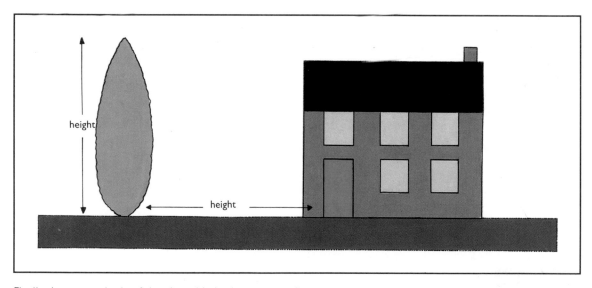

Fig 41   As a general rule of thumb avoid planting any tree closer to a building than its ultimate height to minimize risk of damage to structure and foundations.

Fig 42 Araucaria araucana *(monkey puzzle).
Don't plant this large bold specimen tree too
near the house.*

around the foundations. This leads on to cracked
uneven foundations and eventually, in extreme
cases, to cracked walls too.

Root Pruning

Although the roots of large and semi-mature
conifers occasionally require attention, the need
for root pruning is most likely to arise where
established conifers are wrongly sited and a
move is envisaged. Young conifers can be lifted
and transplanted in a new spot with a reasonable
expectancy of success provided they have been
planted within the last three to five years and are
not over 5–6ft(1.5–1.8m) in height, and provided
they are properly prepared. This involves undercutting – a form of root pruning which is normally best carried out in autumn about twelve
months before lifting and transplanting into new
quarters. *See* pages 42–4 for semi-mature

conifers. For root pruning when planting and
potting *see* page 73.

Topdressing

Generally speaking, topdress around planting
pockets and anywhere else where the topsoil has
been washed away from around plant roots. Aim
to make good the losses before winter.

In the rock garden, deal with each planting
pocket individually. Carefully scrape any surface
chippings to one side. Loosen the top ½in(1cm) of
soil and refirm around the roots before topdressing with lime-free or standard potting compost
as appropriate. Apply sufficient to cover up any
exposed roots. Replace the chippings and sup-
plement as necessary to give a reasonable cover
and prevent wash down of soil in winter. Take
care not to use limestone chippings or other
alkaline aggregate on lime-hating plants.

In the case of small beds, and around single
specimen plants, where the soil is suspected of
being low in organic matter, take the opportunity
to topdress with peat and lightly work it in.

Refirm the roots of any newly set out plants
which have worked loose because of frost or
wind. Topdress to cover any roots exposed using
potting compost or a home-made planting mix,
see page 48. Again take care to use lime-free
mixtures for lime-hating plants.

Mulching

Where beds and borders have been mulched
with bark chips, simply top up with more of the
same, after removing weeds and debris. Otherwise autumn mulching is mainly reserved for
newly set out plants in cold winter areas. Under
these conditions, applications made late in the
year give valuable root protection from frost and
also reduce the intense drying effects of freezing
spring winds.

For plunge beds a generous 2–3in(5–8cm)
thick surface layer of bark, peat or other similar
mulch, scattered over a plunge bed of, for example, conifers, minimizes breakages of pots as well

as providing root protection from frosts. For details of mulching *see* page 67.

Planting

In mild climate areas, and where soil conditions are above average to good, there is much to be said in favour of autumn planting. But in cold winter areas or in very exposed sites, and where soils are heavy, cold and wet in winter, it is advisable to delay planting until spring.

Ensure that all extra heavy nursery stock tree heathers and conifers are adequately supported.

In exposed gardens, provide temporary wind shelter for newly set out plants and do not allow them to dry out. Inspect the supports of existing plants, making sure the stakes are sound. Check that ties are secure and not too tight.

Clipping Over Heathers

As soon as the flowering of summer and autumn blooming heathers is over, clip back the flower spikes by about half to two thirds. This should encourage compact, bushy plants with a succession of flowers and young foliage in the following year. Foliage varieties of *Calluna* are clipped less severely than *Erica* to ensure plenty of 'flower head' interest and foliage colour during the winter months when it is particularly welcome. They can then be given a further trim in spring before new growth begins.

Cut out diseased growths, but this should not be confined to autumn. With heathers and conifers it is best to cut out dead, badly diseased or damaged growths on sight – no matter the time of year. Prune back to sound healthy wood.

Let In Light

Heathers in particular need all the light and air they can get. So it makes good sense to thin out overhanging branches of deciduous trees and shrubs where they are in danger of affecting heathers. Be sure to remove all prunings promptly. If deciduous trees and shrubs look like overcrowding conifers, shorten them back to improve air circulation as well as let in light. Thuja is particularly vulnerable to stagnant air which encourages thuja blight – a disfiguring disease which results in defoliation.

Suckers

Some conifer and rhododendron varieties are grafted onto rootstocks which, on occasion, produce suckers. These inferior and unwanted growths normally arise at about soil level. If left they will weaken, outgrow and take over from the choice variety. Cut out suckers whenever seen as near as possible to their point of origin.

Variegated conifers and some foliage heathers occasionally produce reverted green shoots. Cut them out or they may crowd out the less vigorous variegated foliage.

In newly established beds and borders, once the plants – notably heathers – have had their end-of-season clipping, the final cultivations can go ahead. Where there is any appreciable space between plants, fork over or otherwise loosen the soil to a depth of no more than 4in(10cm). Take care not to disturb the roots, work in summer mulches and hoe off weeds at the same time.

Container Plants

Remove the top ½–¾in(1–2cm) of old potting compost from tubs, sinks and other permanently planted containers which have remained undisturbed for six months or longer. Top up with fresh compost.

Pot on heathers and conifers in small pots if they have been in the same container for twelve months or longer. Move them into larger pots using the same type of compost as before the move. Subsequently shelter them from heavy rain, strong winds and severe frosts. A fine mesh tunnel is ideal for the purpose.

Make up windowboxes and troughs with winter heathers and conifers using the plunge planting technique. *See* page 66.

Plant Raising

Autumn is a good time to start off and increase many members of the heather family, and quite a number of conifers too.

Layering is a fairly easy and normally reliable method of propagation. There is little risk to the parent plant or to the progeny. Layers pinned down now should be rooted and ready for lifting in about twelve to eighteen months. Plants suitable for layering outdoors during autumn include most dwarf or intermediate heathers, plus *Andromeda*, *Cassiope*, *Leucothoe*, *Pieris* and *Vaccinium*.

Given mild, moist conditions and warm soil, plants can be divided successfully during September and October. Pot up the rooted segments and overwinter under a garden frame. *Leucothoe* and *Vaccinium* are increased in this way.

Cuttings offer considerable scope for plant raising. *Arctostaphylos*, *Calluna*, *Cassiope*, various *Erica* as well as *Kalmia* can all be increased from cuttings taken now and rooted under cover. Among the conifers, cuttings of *Chamaecyparis*, *Cryptomeria*, *Juniperus* and Thuja root readily under cover when taken at this time of year.

PROJECTS

Weighing Up the Site

The wider aspects of garden design and layout are beyond the scope of this book. The intention is to focus on the planting, use and care of heathers and conifers within the garden setting. In this context, site assessment simply involves taking a hard look at the garden or individual beds and borders. The object of the exercise is to allocate space for planting, to decide on the nature of the proposed planting and weigh up the existing, and to consider the suitability of the locality as a plant habitat for the successful cultivation of heathers and conifers.

Fig 43 Pinus strobus *'Minuta'* – an uncommon, unusual, compact five-needled pine – well suited to the small garden.

Allocation of Space

To risk stating the obvious the approach should be varied somewhat depending on whether starting from scratch, from a part-made garden, or from a mature one in need of alteration.

To start from scratch, first work out an initial garden plan. In a small garden, assuming there are no major problems on site, this is often easier than it sounds. The advice of preparing detailed plans on graph paper is all very well in theory and essential when dealing with contractors, architects and planners. However, the practical handyperson, with limited time, has to take shortcuts. Provided things are straightforward this is fine – dispense with the graph paper and get outdoors on site.

If a garden is in a new residential development, the chances are that main paths, patio areas, drives and boundaries will have been dealt with. What then remains to decide is which new items are of top priority. Think about drying areas, utility space for dustbins and fuel stores, space for garden shed, greenhouse or garden frame, and lawns and grassed areas. Where any of these features are envisaged, but not yet in existence, it is helpful to peg out their proposed positions using a garden line and pegs. Not only does pegging out direct on site cut out some of the paperwork, but minor problems can be better anticipated. Once the nature and positions of essential hard surfaced areas, structures and lawns have been decided, attention can then be concentrated on the remaining spaces – the planting areas. Consider them well and their suitability for planting, and do not overlook the possible use of container and pocket planting in hard surfaced areas.

The same general principles to determine the allocation of space can usefully be applied to part-made and mature gardens as to new ones. But, as already discussed, the options for new planting are likely to be extremely limited. Open up increased opportunities with the gradual implementation of alterations.

Existing and Proposed Planting

Take stock of all the existing vegetation and planting. Note permanent planting worthy of retention; and note weeds and redundant vegetation for future disposal. Think carefully about the role which both existing and proposed planting is expected to play in future layouts. The checklist of design ideas should help in this respect. (*See* page 31).

Suitability of Site

Some heathers, heather allies and conifers are good natured and adapt reasonably well to a wide range of conditions both above and below ground. Others, such as varieties of *Calluna*, are rather more fussy and quickly become unhealthy

if site and soil are not to their liking. They have at least two strong hates, the first being heavy shade and the second alkaline soil.

It is essential to have 'site assessment' jottings at the ready when choosing plants if a meaningful matching of their needs to the prevailing environmental factors is to take place.

Above Ground

The most telling 'above ground' characteristics which influence plant habitat and behaviour are climate, light and aspect, exposure, wind and shelter, and pollution.

The amount of rainfall can be critical, to some heathers in particular. *Erica ciliaris* and *E. tetralix*, for example, need a moist root run and the sort of moderate to high atmospheric humidity typical of western districts. Incidentally, most conifers enjoy these conditions too. However, lack of rain need not cause any serious problems. This is because there are plenty of heathers as well as conifers which, once established, flourish in the drier eastern and southern areas.

Take note of the variations of light and shade in different parts of the garden. This is of considerable importance when deciding where to plant heathers – most of which are light demanding and shade resentful. Note those parts of the garden which are in full sun for most of the day and aim to reserve these, in part at least, for the heathers. Some parts of the garden are likely to be in near permanent shade – notably those areas under trees, and beds or borders with a north-facing aspect. There are quite a number of conifers which can be expected to grow reasonably well in these shaded spots provided they are otherwise given better than average growing conditions to compensate. Varieties of *Taxus* are amongst the best of conifers for shade. Other parts of the garden are likely to be partially shaded and these areas are suitable for growing a wide range of heather allies and conifers.

A word of caution regarding east-facing positions and the effects of early morning sun common to these sites. Marginally hardy heathers and conifers are best not exposed to early morning sun. The risk is frost damage caused by an over-rapid thaw after overnight freezing. The same applies, but to a lesser extent, to winter flowering heathers and evergreen allies.

Notice which parts of the garden are most exposed to wind, which are well sheltered and which fall somewhere in between. The wind factor is of special significance in coastal districts; in windswept exposed gardens on high ground; and between buildings where the wind tunnelling effect emphasizes the problem.

Fortunately, low-growing and intermediate heathers are particularly well adapted to withstand wind, as are many of their dwarf allies. Be wary with conifers – many need a degree of shelter from cold drying east or north spring winds, especially for the first year or two after planting.

In towns, built-up areas and near industrial sites the fumes, soot and grime are potential hazards to some conifers. Most at risk are probably *Abies* (firs) and *Picea* (spruce). Among the most pollution resistant are *Taxus* and *Chamaecyparis*.

Below Ground

Unfortunately, no one single test can be used to assess the suitability of soil for growing conifers and heathers. Rather it is usual to carry out a few simple tests and observations to reduce the element of risk and guesswork to a minimum.

If rhododendrons and magnolias do well and flourish within the garden, or in neighbouring gardens, then these are encouraging signs. Conversely, if clematis, gypsophila, pinks, carnations, and to a lesser extent rosemary, are obviously at home, then tread warily. These are alkaline lovers, and check the soil pH before planting heathers.

Establish the acidity or alkalinity of the soil. Where the status is unknown or suspected of being alkaline, test the soil. This is because alkaline soils – those with a high lime status – are poisonous to many heathers and heather allies. See individual plant entries for details of alkaline tolerance. For average garden purposes there is no need to buy expensive electronic soil test meters. A simple, low-cost, DIY soil test kit will suffice.

Detailed instructions are supplied with soil test kits. Briefly most follow these lines: a number of soil samples are taken from the planting area, around the anticipated root runs, at a depth of say 6in(15cm). The success of any test depends on the thoroughness of sample taking. Take a number of small samples rather than a few large ones. After mixing up the samples, a small amount of soil is mixed with chemical reagent in solution. There is a colour change appropriate to the acidity or alkalinity of the soil, and the colour of the solution is compared to a test colour card. The results are read off directly against a numerical scale (the pH scale) – pH 7 is neutral. Numbers below 7 indicate acidity and above 7 alkalinity.

Much is said and written about the texture of different types of soil. As far as conifers and heathers are concerned, they can be grown on most soils apart from the extremes of infertile stiff clays and exceptionally shallow soils. Even the problems of stiff clays and exceptionally shallow soils can be overcome in time, given effort and copious amounts of organic matter.

Reasonably good soil drainage is important to heathers and most conifers. Waterlogged soils with plant roots standing in stagnant water are fatal. Be suspicious of low-lying pockets surrounded by higher ground – they are particularly at risk from flooding and waterlogging.

When in doubt, there are two simple tests which can help to pin-point possible drainage problems and so provide clues to their remedies. In free-draining soils, surplus surface rainwater must first penetrate down through the topsoil. And secondly, any surplus subsoil water must be able to escape. For satisfactory growth a minimum 10in(25cm) depth of drained topsoil is considered necessary.

The subsoil water test involves digging an

inspection hole about 12in(30cm) across and of a similar depth. The hole needs to be covered to keep out falling rain – a dustbin lid will do. Inspect the hole during prolonged wet weather. If the water level rises more than 2in(5cm) within the hole, subsoil drainage is necessary.

Surface water penetration testing involves digging or forking over a representative patch of border to a depth of 8in(20cm). Make it at least 2ft(60cm) square, removing weed growth, roots and the like. Then take a few cylinders (spent tin cans with tops and bottoms removed will suffice), and push these into the cultivated area, to a depth of about 4in(10cm). Fill to the rim with water and allow to drain. Then immediately refill with more water. If the water level then drops less than 1in(3cm) in two hours, the soil needs attention to improve the penetration rate.

On sloping ground, soil erosion and landslides are an ever-present hazard, especially in areas of high rainfall. Where slopes are steeper than 1 in 3 (i.e. rise vertically by 1ft(30cm) for every

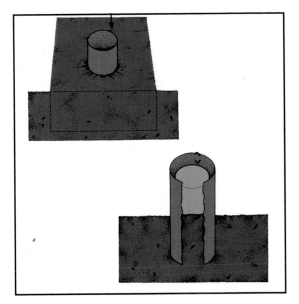
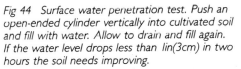

Fig 44 Surface water penetration test. Push an open-ended cylinder vertically into cultivated soil and fill with water. Allow to drain and fill again. If the water level drops less than 1in(3cm) in two hours the soil needs improving.

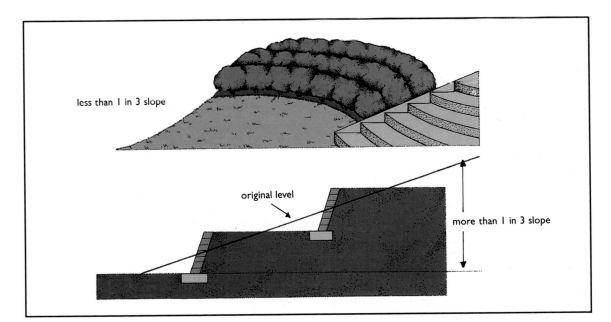

less than 1 in 3 slope

original level

more than 1 in 3 slope

Fig 45 Grassing down and planting across slopes up to 1 in 3. Slopes steeper than this are best terraced.

3ft(90cm) travelled horizontally) it is advisable to have the ground terraced professionally. Slopes less than 1 in 3 can be grassed over or contour planted with shrubs.

Having generally weighed up the site, it is time to progress on to the next phase – implementing ideas.

Site Clearance

No matter whether dealing with a new or mature garden, one of the first jobs is clearing up the site so as to get a clearer picture of the true state of things. When gathering up rubbish, retain anything worth while. Clean stones and rubble, for instance, may come in handy for pathmaking or constructing soakaways.

Where weeds are a major problem, fork out the persistent kinds by their roots as and when soil conditions allow. Weedkillers may be a possibility on large plots, but their use should not be undertaken lightly. First there are the safety risks to children, pets and wildlife to consider, as well as danger to neighbouring land, nearby trees, shrubs and other vegetation. Finally there is a need to allow time for harmful chemical residues to escape before planting can safely begin.

Cut down any garden trees or shrubs that are dead, unthrifty or surplus to requirements – and take time to dig out their roots. Dead stumps, if left to rot away, are a potential source of trouble by acting as host to disease organisms which can then go on to infect healthy plants. When dealing with large trees and shrubs cut off most of the branches but leave a good length of trunk to act as a lever. Dig systematically around the base, keeping subsoil and topsoil separate and severing all the main roots. Eventually it should be possible to lever out the stump and dispose of the remains. Pay extra attention when backfilling large holes over 12in(30cm) in depth. Bottom out with stones or rubble. Then return the subsoil, gradually and evenly, consolidating by treading

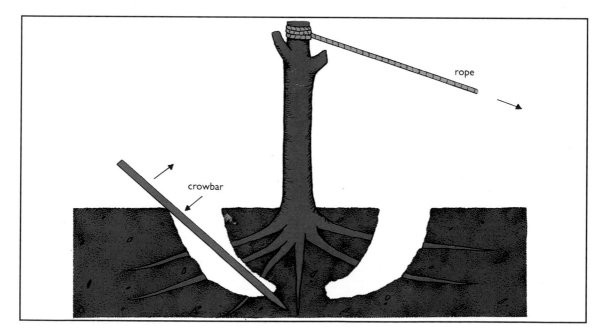

Fig 46 Levering out a tree stump. First sever all main roots. Then attach a rope high up for maximum leverage. Pull on the rope and with the simultaneous help of a crowbar the stump should ease out.

after each 4in(l0cm) layer is added. Finish off with topsoil, bulking up to level with compost, sand or peat.

Never attempt to work the soil when it is overwet or frozen – to do so is to risk long-lasting damage to soil texture.

Finally, when clearing up the site, check on overhanging branches. Where possible it is sound practice to thin these out but bear in mind the general guidelines. Deciduous trees are best pruned in autumn after leaf fall, but with evergreens, late spring or summer are preferable.

Levelling

With experience, minimal levelling out of humps and hollows automatically becomes part of routine digging and subsequent cultivations. Changes in level of a minor nature – up to say 3in(8cm) – do not, as a rule, present any serious difficulties. In practice, when levelling any area of ground, always aim to keep earth moving to a minimum. If possible, try to use the 'cut and fill' technique whereby surplus soil taken from high spots is used as fill material for hollows. But do not fall into the trap of removing all the topsoil from high spots to make up low ground.

Where major levelling or terracing is part of the programme, get qualified on-the-spot advice. This is vital where the work is near to the dwelling or other structures.

When changing levels round existing plants, never be tempted to pile more than 2–3in(5–8cm) of topsoil onto existing root runs, or you will risk root suffocation. When reducing levels do not remove soil too close to the main stem/trunk, or you will risk root exposure and damage. Aim to leave a large collar and drop down levels with a retaining wall if need be (see Fig 47).

Drainage

In the average small garden, there is often not much scope, or need, for anything more than

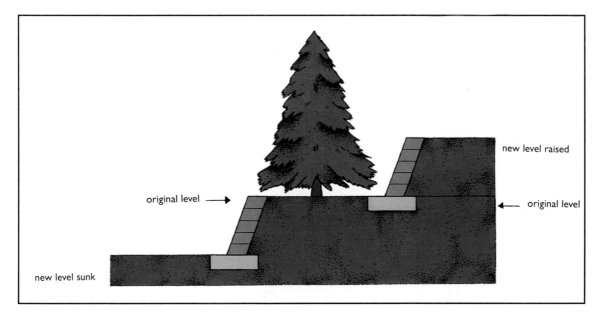

original level ⟶

new level raised

⟵ original level

new level sunk

Fig 47   To change soil levels near trees do not cut away soil too close to the trunk, nor pile soil deeply over the roots. Stabilize banks with retaining walls.

one or two rubble soakaways to deal with subsoil drainage water.

A rubble soakaway, about 3ft(90cm) square and of similar depth, topped over with about 10in(25cm) of topsoil should improve drainage for an area of about 25sq yds(20sq m). The soakaway should be sited in a low spot near the problem area. Before starting to dig, familiarize yourself with the position of services (gas pipes, electric cables and drains). Care should be taken not to interfere with these, and they may lie within a few inches of the surface.

Surface waterlogging and ponding is characteristic of heavy, sticky, clay soils but can also be a problem elsewhere. It maybe owing to, for example, over-compaction or panning (the formation of hard layers of inpenetrable soil). Im provement is achieved by improving soil texture by digging in copious amounts of organic matter at every opportunity. If the soil is inclined to be heavy, work in plenty of coarse sand or grit at the same time — one to two bucketsful per sq yd(m). Ensure the sand is lime-free for heathers. Aim to break up compaction and pans while digging.

Where conditions are very bad, delay planting for twelve months and, in the interim, concentrate on soil improvements. Think in terms of repeating the above treatment three or four times during the year as weather permits.

Wherever possible aim to direct incoming water away from planting areas — very important in low-lying areas. Gulleys are useful for directing rain water from hard surfaced areas like patios to drains. When planting in low-lying areas, it is a good idea to set out hedging and other plants on raised trenches/beds.

Compost Making

No discussion about soil would be complete without some reference to composting.

To make good quality garden compost use the sandwich technique of putting down pest- and disease-free mixed vegetable waste in 4in(10cm) layers. Alternate each layer with a scattering of proprietary compost activator used as the

manufacturers recommend. The easiest way to make good quality compost is to use a proprietary compost bin. They have insulated sides and lids for warmth, they are rain proof and neat.

Deciduous leaves rot down nicely to make leaf mould which is a valuable soil conditioner, nowhere more so than in the heath and heather garden.

One inexpensive way to make leaf mould is to erect a 3ft(90cm) square compound of similar height set on bare earth. Fix chicken wire netting to four corner posts in a well hidden spot. Fill the compound with 4in(10cm) layers as described for composting. But this time alternate wet leaves with a scattering of general fertilizer — a small handful makes an average dressing. Cover over between fillings — plastic sheeting is suitable for the purpose, and prevents wash-out of nutrients and speeds up rotting. Expect the leaf mould to be dark, crumbly and ready for use within about two years.

Moving Existing Conifers

On occasions, a wrongly sited conifer may need moving to a new position, and provided the conifer is not more than about 6ft(1.8m) in height, the roots are accessible and the soil is not too stony, the chances of success are fair. Chances are increased from fair to good if the plants have not been in their present positions for more than three to five years.

The conifer needs to be 'undercut' during autumn, about twelve months before the anticipated move. This encourages the development of a compact, fibrous root system, better able to withstand the move. Dig out a circular trench around the conifer of the width and depth of a spade, leaving a rootball measuring about 20in(50cm) across. Carefully sever any main roots crossing the trench but preserve the fibrous ones. It is essential to backfill the trench quickly to prevent these fibrous roots drying out. Use good quality topsoil for backfilling, enriched with peat and sand if needed. Alternatively use planting mix (see page 48). Water thoroughly to

Fig 48 To undercut a conifer, dig a circular trench around the base and
sever all thick roots exposed. Backfill without delay.

settle the soil. The roots must be kept moist at all
times during the following year, and a spring
mulch helps.

In autumn, twelve months after undercutting,
prepare a planting hole wide and deep enough to
take the new root ball comfortably. Loosen the
sides and bottom out with a 1in(3cm) layer of
well-rotted leafmould, garden compost, or peat.
Spread a good handful of bonemeal over the
organic matter and lightly fork it in to the bottom
of the hole. Water thoroughly, and then water
the conifer as well. Allow it to soak overnight
before disturbing. Spray the foliage with a proprietary anti-wilt preparation as the makers
direct. Carefully tie in any outstretching branches
before wrapping the entire conifer in fine mesh
netting. Tie the netting to secure and minimize
the risk of damage while moving.

Lifting and moving is a job for calm, mild, dull
weather. Have a large, approximately 5ft(1.5m)
square, sheet of heavy gauge plastic at the ready.
This is to work under and around the roots. then
set about digging around the roots, re-excavating

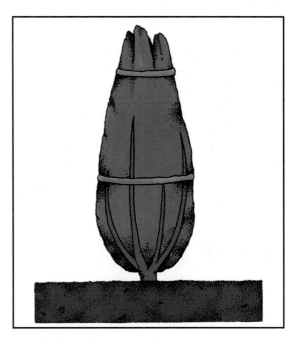

Fig 49 Tie in a multi-stemmed conifer to
prevent branches being damaged during the
move.

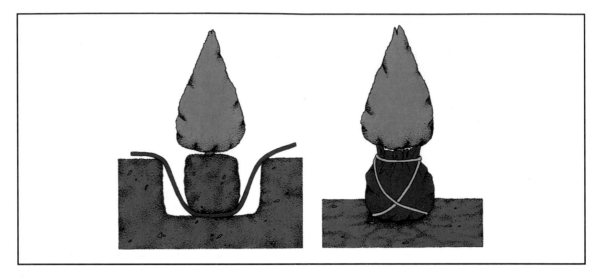

Fig 50   *A year after undercutting, dig around and under the rootball which is then eased onto a plastic sheet. Wrap up the ball in the sheet and tie before attempting to move to new position.*

Fig 51   *To transplant an established conifer move the rootballed conifer into a previously prepared pit. Remove the plastic sheeting. Ensure the top of the rootball is about ¾in(2cm) below the level of the surrounding soil. Backfill with good planting mix and firm.*

the original circular trench and making it a bit wider. Ensure that a rootball of no less than 20in(50cm) across is left. Working from the trench, continue to dig under and around the rootball, until it is possible to roll the conifer gently onto one side and work the plastic part-way underneath. Roll the conifer back, first into an upright position, then onto the opposite side, allowing the plastic to be pulled under and around the rootball. Gently drag the conifer to its new position keeping the rootball intact. Positioned in its new hole, with the best side facing the main viewing point, and with the roots at the same depth as before the move, the conifer is now ready for settling. Ease out the plastic sheet from under the rootball. Backfilling is a two-handed job, requiring one person to steady the conifer and keep it upright, while the other works soil around the roots. Use good topsoil or a prepared planting mixture.

Tread the soil to firm as infilling proceeds. Soak the roots thoroughly and untie the protective wrapping promptly. Protect from drying winds for twelve months, and keep well watered for one to two years.

CHAPTER 3

Winter Scene

Even during the darkest months and shortest days of the year, heathers and conifers can be relied upon to make an impact. In fact, in many a garden, they provide the backbone of winter interest. During mild spells, winter flowering heathers complement well the varied hues of both foliage varieties and conifers. The differing conifer shapes and forms are appreciated to greatest effect when viewed under the crispness of a cold, clear, winter's day, especially when there is snow about.

Because of the adverse weather and tricky soil conditions, scope for working outdoors amongst plants is always somewhat limited at this time of year. It is a case of seizing every favourable opportunity to push ahead with the work.

WINTER CALENDAR

The continuation and completion of various jobs started in autumn should now be of top priority.

1. Remove and dispose of the last of the fallen deciduous leaves.
2. Grub out dead and unwanted trees, shrubs and other plants.
3. In high rainfall areas, check and replenish top-dressings in the rock garden.
4. In cold winter areas, top up bark mulches around newly planted conifers.
5. See to preliminary ground preparations and construction work in advance of planting.
6. Attend to tree supports, especially after high winds.
7. When the thaws come, firm around the roots of newly set out plants which have been loosened by frost heave or wind. Choose a time when the ground is not overwet or sticky.
8. Protect young plants with temporary wind screening in exposed gardens – this is vital with conifers.
9. Test soil drainage. This is an excellent time of year, when the ground is saturated by winter wet, to test the effectiveness of drainage, especially subsoil drainage.
10. Delay any further clipping of heathers until late winter in mild areas, and spring elsewhere.

Knock the snow off trees after heavy falls, and tie in multi-stemmed conifers like yew in areas subject to cold winters or heavy rains. This prevents the spread of branches as a consequence of heavy falls of snow and deluges of driving rain.

Container Plants

Concentrate on protecting plants from wind and frost. Ensure that plants do not dry out during the high winds of winter, and safeguard roots against waterlogging during prolonged wet weather.

Plant Raising

Delay the increase of heathers and conifers apart from sowing seed until spring and the onset of warmer weather. This also applies to plant division, taking cuttings and pinning down layers.

PROJECTS

Some of the project work such as site clearance, levelling and drainage, discussed in the previous chapter as being appropriate to autumn, can of course be undertaken in winter, provided weather and soil conditions allow.

Buying Plants

Always aim to obtain plants in good time – the main planting times being autumn and spring. Where the intention is to grow less common varieties it is important to start shopping around and order early. Delivery may take several weeks and more.

The discerning buyer may well opt for a specialist nursery – they stand the best chance of holding an extensive range of stock though travel is usually involved. With this in mind, there is much to be said in favour of shopping at a local garden centre where plants can be inspected on site. In addition local advice can very often be sought too. When dealing with mail order companies, take care to do business only with established and reputable organizations. Be wary about buying from non-specialist shops where, often, it is variable seed-raised stock which is on offer. The possibility of consequential disappointments, in say five or ten years time when the plants reach maturity, is very real. (See raising from seed, page 87.)

When buying heathers and conifers, it is more important than with many other garden plants, to obtain varieties which are correctly and fully named and labelled.

Appearances can be misleading. Never buy a young conifer on the basis of looks alone. Young plants in their juvenile foliage can look very different when older and wearing their adult greenery, and plant shape and habit can vary naturally with age. Correct labelling provides a guarantee of sorts about what a plant's ultimate characteristics are likely to be.

There is no easy way of knowing if a heather plant is, for example, lime tolerant, nor indeed if a young conifer is a dwarf specimen or a large forest tree other than by checking the varietal name against a reliable reference table or catalogue.

With conifers, and to a lesser extent in the case of heathers, it is worth considering the implications of age and size on maturity.

As a general rule, in an average garden setting, good container-grown, 'standard-size nursery stock' represent a sound choice. Given reasonable care and attention, they should provide an appreciable impact and display within two or three years of planting.

Small pot-grown plants – sometimes referred to as 'lining out stock' – are also a good bet, provided they are healthy, sturdy and well grown. These plants usually work out considerably cheaper than standard-size stock but they take an extra year or two to reach maturity, and need more initial care if losses are to be avoided.

'Extra heavy' or 'advanced' nursery stock are larger than standard nursery stock and provide more or less instant impact. Against this benefit must be weighed the increased cost of the plants, as well as taking into account the fact that conifers 3ft(90cm) in height and over can be slow and tricky to establish. They are also likely to be less well anchored than standard nursery stock in the long term.

If buying plants from garden centres and nurseries they can be inspected before purchase and their condition judged.

Look for good, healthy foliage colour appropriate to the variety. The foliage should be evenly distributed all round and ideally down to soil level. Ignore plants with leafless bare stems as this is indicative of neglect or overcrowding earlier on in life. In the case of conifers, foliage regrowth is unlikely.

Study the branch framework. It should be sturdy, and well formed. For tall tree conifers, the ideal is a single, unforked main stem. Foliage and stems should be free of pests and diseases.

To risk repetition, heathers, conifers and heather allies are all best bought as container-grown stock. Not only is there less chance of setback when planting out, but plants establish more quickly when compared to bare root plants, which sometimes make their way onto the market in prepacks. Aim to obtain plants with a well-developed root system to balance up the top growth.

Look for tell-tale signs of neglect:

1.   The compost is badly dried out and shrinking away from the sides of the container to leave a gap. If so, beware. Badly dried out conifers and heathers invariably shed their foliage.

2.   There is heavy moss and weed growth on the top of the container with roots growing out at the bottom. Is the diameter of the container less than a third of the spread of the plant, or less than a third of the height in the case of tall, slim varieties? These are all signs of neglect, and the plant is obviously suffering and is probably pot bound.

3.   The container is only half-full of compost. In cases like this, the chances are that as the compost has been washed out by rain and irrigation and topdressing has been neglected. The plant is likely to be starved and the growth hard with a weakened root system.

4.   Plants that have obviously been potted recently into largish pots. If so be suspicious, especially if there is movement and the plant wobbles. These plants may have been field-grown and then lifted and potted. Such plants are unlikely to do well and cannot be compared to plants which have been grown in pots all their life.

Buying Containers

Aesthetic considerations apart, there are a few important points to watch:

1.   *Size and shape*   Look for a container with a minimum depth and diameter equivalent to a third shrub height or spread. It takes a lot of compost to sustain a tree or shrub and the container must be large enough to hold sufficient compost for secure root anchorage while acting as a reservoir for nutrients and moisture. If containers are to be wind-firm, they must be wider than they are tall. Look for near vertical sides to make the job of repotting and topdressing, as well as day to day watering easier.

Fig 52   Thuja plicata 'Rogersii' – a slow growing, rounded, hardy thuja. Good both in containers and when direct planted.

2.   *Insulation*   Plant roots are vulnerable to the ravages of heat and cold when grown in containers. Look for good insulation, or be prepared to use fibre liners. Wood is a good insulator, concrete and simulated stone are reasonable, terracotta fair, but inexpensive plastics are poor.

3.   *Drainage*   It is important to have plenty of drainage holes in the base of containers, otherwise you risk waterlogging and root suffocation during winter.

4.   *Metal and concrete containers*   Lime-hating plants are particularly at risk from metal or alkali poisoning if their roots come into direct contact with unprotected metal, concrete, simulated stone or alkaline ceramics. There are several ways round the problem. Liners can be used to provide a physical barrier between the roots and the container. Alternatively opt for pre-treated inner surfaces which eliminate the dangers of

toxicity. Containers can also be satisfactorily treated before planting using a safe, proprietary, horticultural sealing compound.

Buying Composts

The present choice of compost is usually between soil-based, peat-based or modern multi-composts, which are made up of equal parts soil-based and peat-based compost. However, the compost market is a rapidly changing scene, and the single most important factor when dealing with lime-hating plants is always to buy lime-free mixtures.

For heather, conifer, shrub and tree growing, soil-based mixtures are the easiest to manage. The general-purpose type of soil-based compost is very popular and certainly the easiest to obtain, and in many quarters it is superseding the traditional John Innes soil-based type of mixture. This is unfortunate because John Innes mixtures are virtually infallible and excellent for beginners, largely because of their fertilizer content. They are made up in varying strengths – No 2 being good for most potting purposes, while the richer No 3 is well suited to more vigorous plants. When using the so-called 'general-purpose' mixtures, the fertilizer content needs adjusting and there is room for error until experience is gained.

Many peat-based mixtures lose their texture after about six months, and this makes them more tricky to manage. Another point to consider is weight, and being lightweight there is more likelihood of containers being blown over when filled with peat-based composts than soil-based. In fact inexpensive plastic containers rely on the weight of compost for stability.

Preparing a Peat Bed Compost

The possibility of growing lime-hating plants in peat beds has been discussed on page 27, and in this context equal parts lime-free general-purpose soil-based compost and peat make a good growing medium. Add a small handful each of bonemeal and general fertilizer to each bucketful of mixture, and ensure thorough mixing by layering up in a heap and then turning the heap at least three times. It is very important to obtain an even distribution of fertilizer and peat throughout the mix.

Preparing a Planting Mixture

At the time of purchase, most bought-in conifers and heathers are growing in containers of peat-based compost, and when planted out in average garden soil, the roots find difficulty in breaking out of the peat and into the soil. To help avoid a setback, planting mixtures are used for backfilling. They contain a higher percentage of peat than garden soil, and when worked in between the peaty rootball and surrounding soil the change from one rooting medium to another becomes more gradual and thus more acceptable to the plant.

Proprietary soil-based composts make ideal planting mixtures but where supplies of good topsoil are available, home-made mixtures are cheaper. Mix three bucketsful of topsoil to one bucketful each of peat and coarse sand. *See* peat bed mix above for fertilizer rates and mixing.

Winter Care of Container Plants

During the winter months both containers and plants are at risk. Wind, wet and frost are all responsible for damage and injury. Terracotta and glazed ceramic containers are not reliably frost resistant and should be used as the manufacturers recommend. Some need to be moved under cover during winter. Lightweight, inexpensive plastics are suspect too as they can turn brittle and crack during prolonged frost.

Minimize the dangers to overwintering plants by:

1. Moving containers, plus plants, up against a south or west wall for shelter and warmth.
2. Avoiding exposure of plants to early morning sun. This is a typical problem common to east-facing sites where rapid thawing after overnight

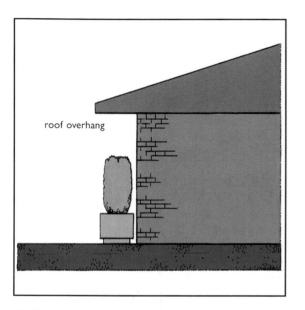

Fig 53 In autumn move hardy container plants against a south or west wall, beneath a roof overhang, for winter warmth and to keep off rain.

frost can cause blackening and scorching of leaves, buds and flowers. If there is no practical alternative other than to stand plants against east-facing walls, then provide some form of shade early in the morning, and so allow plants to thaw out slowly. Fine mesh netting works well.

3. Providing temporary wind shelter where container plants are very exposed and liable to wind damage. Young plants are particularly at risk. Fine mesh netting on a light but secure frame to provide all-round protection will suffice.

4. Ensuring that containers are well drained and plants are not standing in water. In high rainfall areas consider fitting a plastic container cover to keep off winter rains. Once fitted, make sure that things do not get too dry under the cover. Alternatively, move the container under a building or wall overhang.

Take extra precautions to protect the roots of container plants and this is vital if they are grown

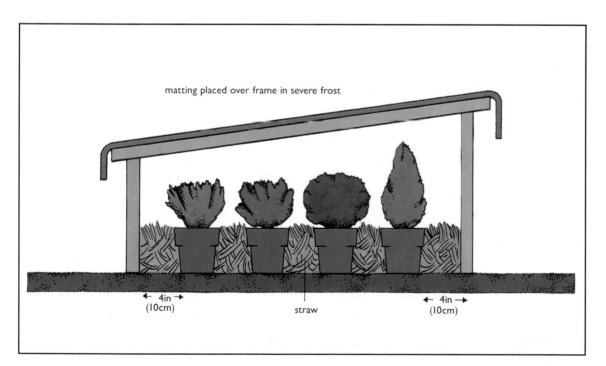

Fig 54 Pack the pots of young plants in straw for protection against frost when overwintering in a garden frame.

in cold winter areas. Roots are particularly vulnerable to injury during periods of prolonged severe frost. Where containers stand above ground level, roots have to contend with frost striking in from the sides as well as the top of the rootball. A comparable plant, set out in the ground or plunge planted, has only the top of the rootball exposed.

Large containers can be protected by simply building up a collar of straw or leaves around the roots and container, held in place with such as netting. However, from the appearance point of view, where containers are not too heavy, the practice of setting a smaller container inside a larger one has much to commend it. The space between inner and outer container is then packed with straw for insulation.

Smaller containers can conveniently be plunge planted into a larger container, or bed, for protection. In the case of young plants over-wintering under a garden frame, pack the pots in straw. leave a minimum 4in(10cm) thickness of straw between the outermost pots and the sides of the frame, (see Fig 54). In very severe weather place sacking or a mat over the frame at night for extra protection.

Making a Rock Mound

Few will disagree that a well-designed and properly constructed rock garden provides an ideal setting for heathers and conifers. Unfortunately, since many gardens – new as well as established ones – are flattish, this very often remains a pipedream. The best solution very often is to settle for a compromise, which can take the form of a simple raised bed or a series of raised beds. Either way the aim is to form a sort of rocky

Fig 55   A collection of dwarf conifers arranged naturally on a rockery.

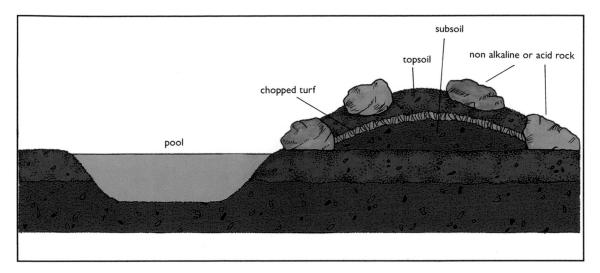

Fig 56 Making a rocky mound with excavated soil from a pool nearby
helps to keep earth moving to a minimum.

outcrop. One practical way to achieve these ends, with a minimum of earth moving and without necessarily incurring great expense, is to create the raised mound in conjunction with a garden pool. The excavated material from the pool is then used to provide the bulk of the fill needed to build the mound.

Peg out the position of the pool with a roughly corresponding area of pleasing outline for the mound. Carefully strip off any turf in 12in(30cm) squares from the pool area. Place it to one side for neatening off later when the construction work is completed. Next dig out and stack the topsoil near the mound area. Finally dig out the subsoil from the pool area to the required depth and shape as decreed by the prefabricated pool liner. Spread the subsoil over the mound area, having first skimmed off any turf. It is important to firm by treading after each 4in(10cm) layer of soil has been added. Top over the subsoil with any available turf chopped up into small pieces. At this stage take some good sized pieces of non-alkaline rocks and strategically position them around the outer edges of the mound to give the sought after 'rocky' appearance, and to contain the topsoil/planting mix.

Prepare a good planting mixture by supplementing the topsoil with peat, sand and fertilizer. Spread the planting mix over the mound area packing it firmly behind the rock at the edges. Aim for a 10in(25cm) minimum depth of planting mix to support dwarf conifers and heathers. Ensure that the mound is slightly raised centrally so as to shed rainwater. If desired, another layer of rocks and planting mix can be added to form a central high plateau with terrace surround.

Making a Rocky Peat Pocket

Since the present cost of peat together with a concern for the conservation of peat bogs puts a traditional peat bed out of the reach of many gardeners, a rocky peat pocket could be considered as a good alternative. As with a peat bed, a rocky peat pocket answers the problem of growing lime haters in gardens with alkaline soils.

Mark out the proposed area and edge around with non-alkaline rocks, as for the mound. Bottom out with imported clean builders rubble. Dust over liberally with flowers of sulphur to neutralize any tendency towards alkalinity. Then build up with peat bed mix (see page 48). Aim for a minimum planting depth of 10in(25cm) but this time take care not to consolidate the peat bed mixture or risk destroying the texture.

Do not construct a rocky peat pocket, or peat bed for that matter, at a low point in the garden.

51

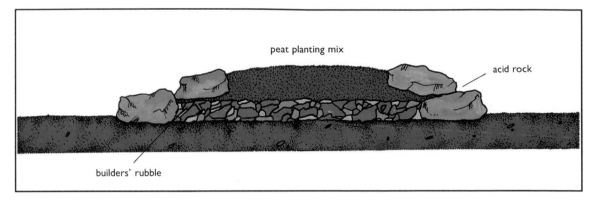

Fig 57   A rocky peaty pocket provides the answer to growing lime haters on alkaline soils.

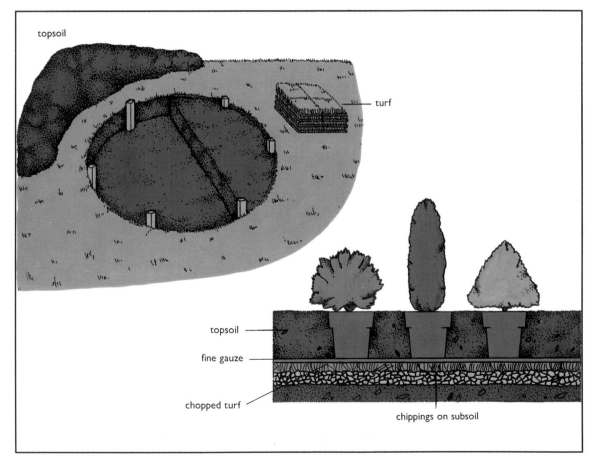

Fig 58   Making a plunge bed. Left: a part-excavated bed with turf removed. Right: a section of prepared bed with plants plunged in topsoil.

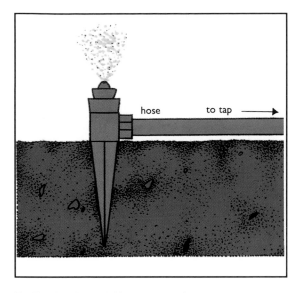

Fig 59 A spike sprinkler connected to a tap
via a hosepipe and set in the plunge bed
simplifies watering.

The danger is that drainage water from surrounding higher ground is going to wash into it and quickly destroy the acid nature.

Any peat bed or pocket is going to need regular topping up with acid peat planting mixture to maintain a suitable pH for healthy growth of lime haters.

Making a Plunge Bed

In the average private garden, a plunge bed is something of a rarity, and it is true that in the context of growing heathers and conifers, a plunge bed is mainly of interest to the collector of dwarf and slow-growing conifers. But there are a few other advantages. For instance for anyone intending to move home, the contents of a plunge bed are easily transported, plunged plants do not blow about and are better protected from frost.

Take time to prepare a plunge bed properly, or be prepared to face problems later on.

First select a suitable area. Site a plunge bed out of the drips of trees and in a spot which is neither too shaded nor exposed to freezing winds, and avoid wind tunnel positions between buildings.

Peg out the area and strip off any turf. Dig out the topsoil to a minimum depth of 8in(20cm) and

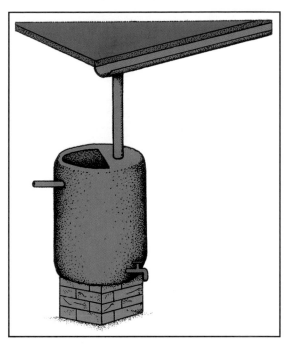

Fig 60 A rainwater butt, fed from a gutter
will prove invaluable for trapping rainwater –
especially when growing lime-hating plants.

stack it to one side near the bed. To ensure good drainage, spread a 2in(5cm) layer of chippings and rake level. Cover the chippings with chopped up turf or, in the absence of turf, fine mesh netting. This will prevent the topsoil working its way down in amongst the chippings and impeding drainage.

Space the pots out on the netting or turf. Start at one end and bury the pots up to their rims in the topsoil. Work systematically across the bed, arranging the plants and burying the pots. For large beds of over 4ft(1.2m) in width, leave spaces for laying stepping stones. This makes it easier to work amongst the plants.

A useful labour-saving tip is to fix permanent spray nozzles for watering the plunge bed. It is important to make sure that the hose nozzles and connections can be drained during winter (see Fig 59). It is also a good idea to take steps to ensure a reserve water supply. One or two water butts, fed from guttering from a shed roof is a good start. Trapping rainwater is strongly advocated when growing lime-hating plants in any event.

53

CHAPTER 4

Spring Scene

Spring signals the start of greatly increased activity in the garden, and the signs are there for all to see. With lengthening days and warmth from the sun, plant growth visibly quickens. Unfortunately, so does weed development!

Fig 61 Erica arborea – *this is one of the finest and hardiest of the spring flowering tree heaths.*

In a successful conifer and heather garden, there should be plenty of colour and interest at the moment, especially in mild districts. Spring flowering heathers are in full bloom, along with the last of the winter varieties. Dwarf and intermediate varieties are well backed up with tree heathers, amongst which *Erica arborea* 'Alpina' is outstanding. This is a particularly fine variety, of tall stature, its masses of sweetly scented, dainty white flowers cannot go unnoticed – they are carried in long spires, midst bright green foliage.

Many heather allies also put on a good display of flowers at this time of year. Worthy of special mention are the dainty pink flowered *Andromeda* and the rose-purple *Kalmia polifolia*. They contrast well with the white flowers of *Cassiope* and *Pieris*. The pink and white flowered *Arctostaphylos* and *Vaccinium* bloom in spring and then go on to provide a bonus of berry colour later in the year.

Dwarf rhododendrons are around to offer contrast in both colour and texture. Yellow is introduced along with shades of pink, purple, red, cream and white. Yellow as a flower colour is very much in the minority amongst heathers and heather allies.

As old foliage colourings give way to new, this is the season when conifers and foliage heathers take on fresh and brighter shades of greens and golds, though a lot depends on variety.

SPRING CALENDAR

Begin the new season with a good clean up, lightly cultivating bare earth to break up surface crusting and kill seedling weeds.

Fig 62   Work dry fertilizer into the surface soil around established
conifers using a Dutch hoe or cultivator.

Recheck firmness and topdressing of all newly set out plants and refirm any loosened by wind or frost. Cover over any exposed roots with fine topsoil or planting mixture. Work dry fertilizer into the surface soil around established conifers and water in. Alternatively, feed with liquid fertilizer. Topdress planting pockets and make good areas of chippings washed away by winter rains.

Water and mulching. Keep all newly set out plants well watered until established, and apply mulch to moist soils. Spray over newly planted conifers and tree heathers with clean rainwater, drenching the foliage thoroughly. This is a job for the evening during dry warm or windy weather.

Wait until the frost is completely out of the ground, and the soil has dried out a little, before continuing the preparatory work of beds, borders and other planting areas in readiness for planting. This is also a good time to see to ground clearance, levelling, drainage and other construction work.

This is the main planting season for heathers, conifers and heather allies.

Anti-wilt sprays are beneficial if applied before or immediately after planting and use them as the makers recommend. They are of particular significance when setting out extra heavy stock or when dealing with gardens exposed to cold, drying winds, or when moving established conifers to new positions.

Take steps to safeguard newly planted hedges from the attentions of dogs. If dogs are allowed to urinate on the lower leaves, loss of foliage is inevitable. Protect new plants with temporary shelter from cold, drying spring winds in exposed windswept gardens. Use fine mesh netting (*see* Fig 63 for details).

Cut out any dead, damaged, badly diseased or galled shoots or branches to prevent the spread of trouble.

Clip over autumn flowering heathers such as *Erica ciliaris*, *E. cinerea* and *E. vagans* along with foliage varieties. Deal with winter and spring flowering kinds as they finish blooming. Continue to cut out suckers from conifers and rhododendrons as they arise, and promptly remove any reverted green shoots from variegated heathers and conifers.

55

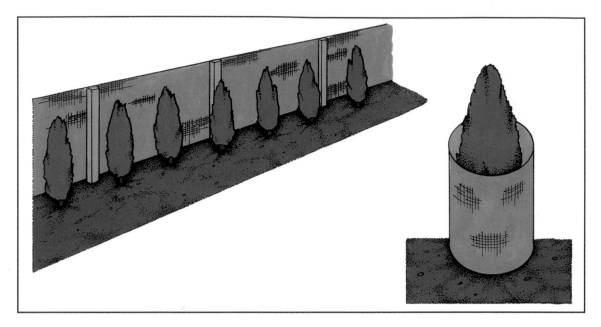

Fig 63   Fine mesh netting can provide useful protection against dogs, as well as wind, for a new conifer hedge.

Crown thin conifers to prevent branch over-crowding (*see* Chapter 5), and where necessary, remove outworn lower branches as part of a crown raising programme. This is most likely to

Fig 64   Crown thinning involves the removal or shortening of not more than about one-third of all the branches – see broken lines.

be called for with ageing conifers such as pine. Spring is also a good time to thin out evergreens where they cause excessive shade to the detriment of heathers and other sun-loving plants.

Container Plants

During mid- to late spring, as the weather begins to get warmer and the danger of damaging frost recedes, start to move container plants from their winter shelter to summer quarters, and you can also remove any straw or other insulation materials.

Where plants are not to be disturbed by potting on or repotting, give the containers a good clean then topdress. It is normal to pot on young plants every year and move older plants in alternate years.

To pot on move plants into a larger sized container if they have not yet reached maturity and growth is to be encouraged. The same rules apply no matter whether plants are potted direct or plunge planted. Repot plants back into

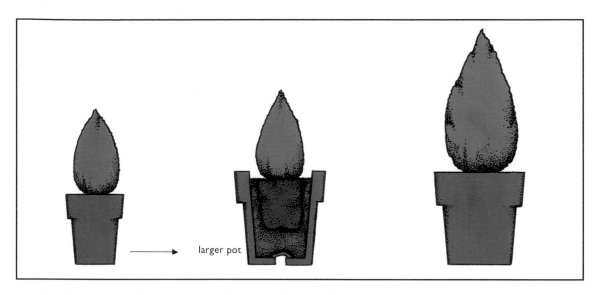

Fig 65 Potting on into a larger container is the norm where the aim is an increase in plant size.

the same sized container where plants need to be restrained in size.

Plant up new containers, including liners, and rearrange plunge planted schemes as necessary. Change over permanently planted liners of such as windowboxes where for example winter flowering heathers are exchanged for summer flowering kinds. As the season advances, gradually increase watering and syringe over container-grown conifers. Feed with weak, balanced liquid feed at fortnightly to three weekly intervals, starting about a fortnight after topdressing or three weeks to a month after potting.

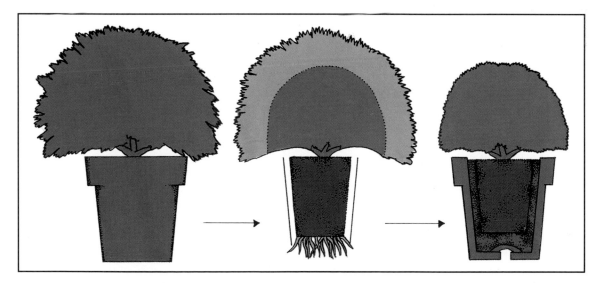

Fig 66 Repotting into the same size of container is normal practice when the intention is to restrict plant size, yet keep them healthy. Some pruning of roots and shoots is involved.

PROJECTS

Getting the ground ready to receive plants is a job which merits a great deal more attention than it is often afforded. If it is worth spending time and money on buying good plants, it surely makes good sense at least to aim to give them the right root conditions for satisfactory future growth and development. Soil improvement is at best difficult and at worst well nigh impossible once the land is planted up. Bear in mind that the ground is occupied for a long time after planting. Calculate on up to fifteen years or more in the case of heathers and heather allies, and hopefully for a lifetime plus with conifers. It is also important to realize at the outset that heathers, and to a lesser extent conifers, are rather more fussy about soil conditions than many other plants.

The aim when preparing soil for planting, should be all about creating a reasonable root environment. Soil factors which have the greatest influence on healthy growth and development are warmth, air, moisture, plant nutrients, depth, pests, diseases and pollution.

In practice, generous applications of organic matter in the form of peat, garden compost, leaf mould or manure help to achieve the right balance of soil air and moisture. In turn this has a bearing on soil temperature. Badly drained, fine textured, wet clay soils contain excess moisture and too little soil air. They are cold and slow to warm up in spring, though regular and generous dressings of organic matter bring about noticeable improvements. At the other end of the scale, coarse, open textured, sandy, gravelly soils contain excess air and too little moisture. They dry out quickly in drought and become hot and inhospitable to plant roots during summer. Again copious amounts of organic matter make life more bearable for plants, and manuring and feeding build up and replenish nutrient levels in the soil. Increasing the depth of fertile topsoil by manuring and cultivation not only helps to ensure greater reserves of nutrients and moisture but also ensures better anchorage, more vigorous root development and an increased drought resistance. Finally, keeping

soil pests and diseases in check and preventing pollution goes a long way towards healthy growth.

The precise way to go about preparing the soil for planting will depend, in the main, on three factors:

1. The nature of the planting. Is it to be in bed, border, peat bed, plunge bed, rock garden pocket, grassed area or as hedging?
2. The relation of existing soil depth and condition to the needs of the proposed plants. Heathers for example, need less depth of fertile top soil than medium to tall conifers.
3. The question of climate, particularly rainfall and wind. For instance, in high rainfall areas, and in very exposed gardens it is normally advisable to adapt general guidelines of preparations and planting techniques to suit local conditions.

When to Prepare the Ground

As with most gardening jobs, the timing of operations depends to a large extent on individual circumstances. Consideration of the conditions of the soil and site, the weather, the availability of time and materials, and the degree of urgency to push ahead with planting, all have a part to play. However, since the favoured planting times are spring and autumn, final preparations need to be completed by then.

Well-drained, light to average soils can be cultivated at most times of year provided the weather is fine and the ground neither over wet nor frozen. Heavy clay soils, on the other hand, are much more demanding. They are inclined to be sticky and difficult to work when wet, and impossible to cultivate when dry as they set like concrete and crack badly. Frequently, autumn is the only time of year when the moisture content of heavy clay soils allows satisfactory working. In any event, clay soils are much improved by digging in autumn and then being left to mellow over winter. Because of the weathering action of alternating wind and frost, wetting and drying, they are usually in a reasonable state to work down into a satisfactory tilth in time for spring planting.

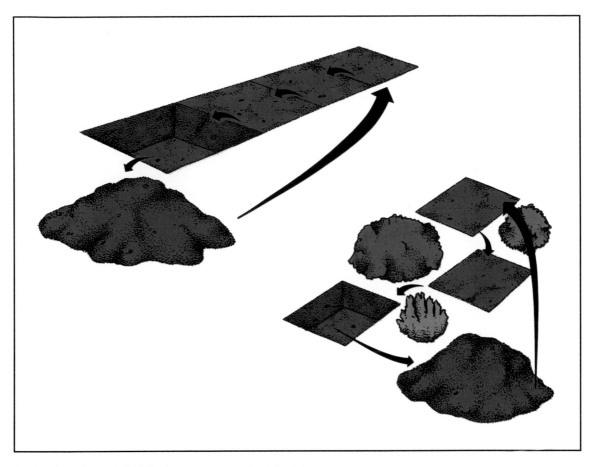

Fig 67   Strip digging in 2ft(60cm) squares to required depth is a
convenient method of working in small spaces. Soil from the first square
is used to fill in the last.

Preparing Beds and Borders

In spite of all the modern trappings attached to
the gardening scene, the best results are still
usually obtained by following sound and proven
traditional practices. There is, of course, room
for minor modifications as experience is gained.

Assuming that the ground is clear of major
obstructions, drains freely, is reasonably level,
and the area is marked out, work can begin.
Where the soil is more or less average and, unlike
clay, does not present undue problems of texture
proceed along the following lines.

Aim to dig the soil to a minimum depth of
8–10in(20–25cm) in preparation for heathers and
conifers. Increase the depth to 12in(30cm) in the
case of taller conifers. When digging in fairly confined spaces in small gardens, one easy method
of working is to dig the ground in 'squares' of
convenient size. Starting at a convenient point,
usually at one end, dig out a square of say 2ft×2ft
(60cm×60cm). Take it down to the required
minimum depth. Stack the soil to one side. Fork
the bottom, breaking up the soil to a minimum
depth of 8in(20cm). When preparing for conifers,
spread a bucketful of well-rotted manure, garden
compost or leaf mould evenly over the area. For
heathers substitute half a bucketful of peat.

Proceed by taking out a second square of soil
and infilling the first square with the excavated
soil. Repeat the forking of the base and the
manure/peat applications. Continue to take out
squares in succession, filling the last with soil from
the first (see Fig 67).

Where planting is more or less imminent, start by breaking down large lumps with the back of the fork and then rake level. When preparing to plant heathers and dwarf conifers fork a bucketful of peat per sq yd(m) into the top 3in(8cm) of soil. Immediately prior to planting any shrub, always begin by hoeing or raking in a handful of bonemeal per sq yd(m). If the soil seems very puffy and spongy, firm by treading heel to toe fashion and rake level once more. But, as with any groundwork, never attempt this when the soil is wet or frozen or you risk ruining the texture.

Lime should be withheld when preparing planting mixtures for heathers and their allies. But where the soil is very acid, with a pH of 5 or below, a dressing of lime would be beneficial to conifers and other non-heather plants. A handful per sq yd(m) of ground limestone, applied in late autumn or winter, is usually quite adequate. Dust the lime evenly over the soil surface and then leave to allow winter rains to wash it into the ground.

For heavy clay soils dig over beds and borders in squares during autumn or early winter working in peat or manure as before. Leave the soil to weather and break down naturally during the winter months. In spring, once the ground is dry enough to work, apply a bucketful of peat, plus one or two bucketsful of coarse sand or fine lime-free grit, and a scattering of bonemeal per sq yd(m).

Where the cost of peat is prohibitive, substitute well-rotted garden compost, leaf mould or manure as a good second best alternative. working from planks, to avoid undue soil compaction, lightly work the peat grit and bonemeal into the topsoil to improve the texture. Clay soils must be allowed to settle naturally — never attempt to tread.

In high rainfall districts, standing water at the base of plants presents a particular risk. However, this problem can be largely overcome by ensuring that plants are set out on such as rocky mounds or by raising beds above the surrounding soil.

Preparations for Hedging

Without doubt, the most satisfactory way of preparing the ground for hedging is the 'trench' method. Dig and manure in 2ft(60cm) wide squares of 12in(30cm) depth, or some prefer to take out a continuous trench, and although this allows the bottom to be forked and manured in one operation, it involves the double handling of excavated topsoil. It also has the added disadvantage of finding somewhere to put the excavated soil in small gardens. Allow a handful of bonemeal per yd(m) run of trench. Rake and firm as before.

Preparation of Planting Pits and Pockets

The main alternative to planting in groups in beds and borders is to set out individual plants in pits and pockets. Specimen conifers and tree heathers are best treated in this manner no matter whether planted in grassed areas or in beds and borders.

1. Mark out an area at least twice as wide as the rootball.
2. When planting in grass remove the turf and stack to one side.
3. Dig out a hole, twice as wide and half as deep again as the rootball. Keep the dark topsoil separate from the paler and less fertile subsoil.
4. Loosen up the bottom and sides of the hole — the prongs of a garden fork are useful for the purpose.
5. Where there is turf available, turn the sods upside down in the bottom of the hole and chop up into small pieces. In the absence of turf, bottom out the hole with a 1–2in(3–5cm) layer of well-rotted manure, compost or leaf mould for conifers. Make it a 1in(3cm) layer of peat for tree heathers.
6. Largish conifers may need support. If so, hammer in a stake (see page 64).
7. Scatter a small handful of bonemeal over the chopped turf, manure or peat. Cover the

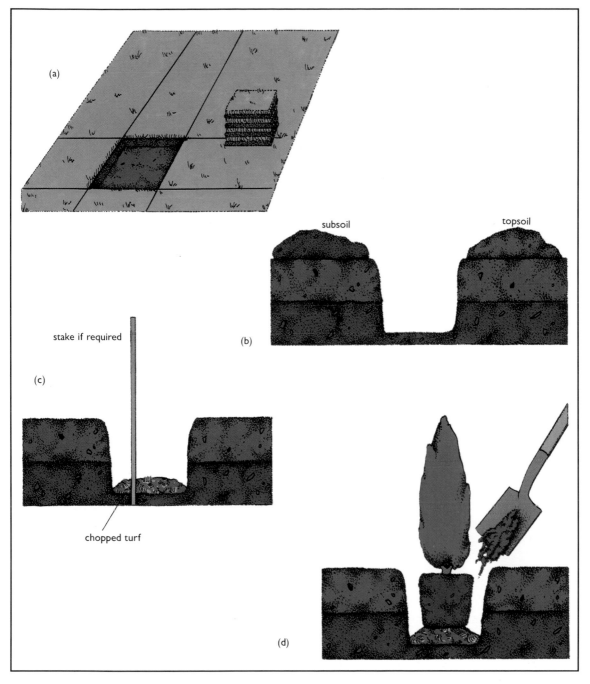

Fig 68   Pit planting in grass step by step: (a) Mark out an area at least twice as wide as the rootball. Remove and stack the turf nearby. (b) Dig out the hole to a depth half as deep again as the rootball, keeping topsoil and subsoil separate. Fork up the bottom and loosen the sides with a fork. (c) Line the bottom with chopped turf or manure and hammer in a stake if needed. Scatter a handful of bonemeal plus planting mix. (d) Try the plant for depth. Remove its container, tease out roots, backfill and firm. Tie to support as necessary.

bonemeal with a few handfuls of planting mixture (*see* page 48).

When setting out smaller plants in isolated pockets, the same rules apply. Take out holes twice as wide and half as deep again as the container and proceed as before.

GETTING PLANTS READY

Root dryness is a very serious and common problem and can be fatal with newly set out plants. The answer is to ensure that the rootball is thoroughly moist at planting time, and then kept well watered until the plants are established. This involves watering during dry spells throughout the first growing season at least and longer if need be. The type of peat composts used for raising and growing on heathers and conifers are very difficult to re-wet if once dried out, either before or after planting. One almost infallible way to ensure thorough wetting prior to planting is to stand the plants in water, up to the rims of their containers, for about four hours. It is important to allow about thirty minutes for surplus water to drain away before disturbing the roots.

Pick over each plant before planting, trimming any straggly or misplaced shoots. In the case of heathers, drastically shorten back any flowered shoots. Tree heathers sometimes fork to develop two or more main stems. If this has happened, reduce to one, leaving the strongest and straightest to grow up. If conifers or tree heathers are untidy and out of shape try corrective pruning at this stage but avoid exposing bare stems by cutting back beyond new growth.

Tie in any new stems which are growing out of shape. Use soft green inconspicuous twine and remove the twine after a year or so by which time the wood should have stiffened in place.

Spray all but the smallest conifers and heathers with proprietary wilt preparations when planting in exposed gardens.

Gently tie in the branches of varieties of spreading conifers, and encase in fine mesh netting. This temporary protection prevents damage during, and makes for easier, planting.

Make sure that plants are correctly labelled for future reference. Never rely on memory.

PLANTING IN SITU

At the risk of stating the obvious, double check that each plant is in its correct place. Make sure, for example, that no vigorous tree conifer is set nearer to buildings and structures than a distance equal to at least its ultimate height. Do not set any plant closer to a wall than 12in(30cm). The risk is unacceptable root dryness and damage to the wall.

Mark out each planting position. Take care that plants are not placed too close together. Be guided by the size and spacings indicated in the individual plant entries in Chapter 7, and make allowances for temporary fillers. For group plantings aim to ensure that dwarf plants are placed in front of tall ones. Mistakes can easily be made, and it is the ultimate height that matters, not the height of the plants at the time they are set out.

Mild, calm, dull and showery weather is ideal for planting. Get everything to hand before starting to plant so minimizing the risk of having to leave plants at some vulnerable stage with their roots exposed. Roots must be protected against drying out at all times during the planting process. Have some damp newspapers to hand for covering over if need be. Plant roots are most at risk during windy, or sunny, weather.

Spade Planting

To plant in a ready dug pit or pocket (*see* page 60) try the hole for size by lowering the plant complete with container, gently into the hole. If necessary, adjust the size of the hole to ensure that the rootball is about half the diameter of the planting pit and about two thirds its depth. Part fill the hole with planting mixture to about a third its depth. Then, in all but periods of very wet weather, water thoroughly. On average soils, think in terms of one or two watering cans per hole. Allow surplus water time to drain away.

With the plant positioned close to the edge of the planting pit, remove the container. It helps to roll rigid pots two or three times from side to side to loosen the rootball from the container sides. The rootball can then be forced out, intact, by pushing a stick up from the bottom, via the drainage holes. Cut floppy plastic or fibre pots vertically up both sides taking care not to damage plant roots in the process. Then simply peel away the pot remains.

Having removed the container, gently tease out some of the potting compost with a pointed stick, along with any drainage material from the base. While aiming to keep the main rootball intact, ease some of the outermost roots away from the rootball so that they fall free. Trim back any damaged roots to sound tissue.

Position the plant in the pit, with the rootball comfortably resting on the planting mixture and making sure that the best side of the plant is facing the main viewing point. At this stage, the top of the rootball should be slightly lower than the surrounding soil level. Spread out the freed roots carefully and then backfill around the rootball with planting mixture or fine sandy topsoil well enriched with peat. Firm as filling proceeds.

Basin and Mound Planting

On very light, quick-draining, sandy soils in dry areas, plants should be set out slightly deeper than the norm and the surrounding soil should be dished slightly so as to form an encircling ridge. Rain and irrigation water is then caught and directed towards the roots (see Fig 69). On these light soils hedging plants are best set out in 2–3in(5–8cm) deep, flat-bottomed furrows.

Conversely, on low-lying wet soils, in high rainfall areas, plants should be set out on slight mounds – about 3in(8cm) above the surrounding soil. In the case of hedging, make a continuous raised ridge.

Trowel Planting

Trowel planting is reserved, in the main, for setting out plants like dwarf heathers, diminutive heather allies and dwarf conifers from small pots. The method of working follows very much the same lines as spade planting but on a lesser scale. Basically, excavate planting holes wide enough and sufficiently deep to take the rootball comfortably.

The golden rule is to plant deep enough and sufficiently firmly. The top of the rootball must

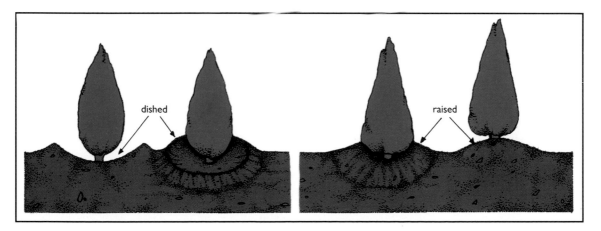

Fig 69   Basin and mound planting. On quick-draining soils in dry areas, plant slightly deeper, and dish the soil. On wet soils in high rainfall areas, plant on a slight mound.

not be set any higher than the surrounding soil – the risk is exposed roots as the soil is inevitably washed and eroded away. Packing planting mixtures around the roots acts as a safeguard on sloping ground. Use a reversed trowel handle to ram the compost home but do not firm so hard as to damage the roots and destroy soil texture.

IMMEDIATE AFTERCARE AND SUPPORTS

As soon as plants are set out in the ground, water them thoroughly to settle the soil around the roots and ensure moist ground in the immediate vicinity. Follow the watering by mulching, and mulch generally to prevent drying out in spring and summer. Mulch for winter protection where necessary (see individual plant entries in Chapter 7). Spray over plants in the evenings during dry warm or windy weather using pure rainwater. Conifers and tree heathers are most at risk. Provide temporary shelter in exposed gardens until established.

Provided that nothing larger than standard sized nursery stock is planted, little should be needed by way of plant supports. Exceptions may arise in the case of tree heathers and conifers planted in very open or exposed gardens. In these situations a stout cane, pushed into the soil near, but not actually into the rootball, will serve the purpose well. Tie in with soft twine.

Advanced, extra heavy stock need something more substantial if they are to be secured against high winds, as do established conifers which have been moved. Stick to the time-honoured, traditional method of using a single timber stake, pre-treated with safe horticultural preservative. This is eminently suitable for a single stem conifer of fairly open habit like Cedrus. For a 6ft(1.8m) extra heavy conifer, use a 7ft(2m) long stake of minimum 1½in(4cm) thickness. Hammer this home, into the planting hole, slightly off centre, before the tree is finally set in position. Allow for about one third the length of any stake to be below ground. Once the conifer is planted and

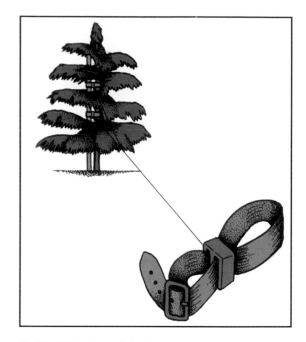

Fig 70 With the traditional single stake method, fasten the tree to the stake with two adjustable ties complete with spacers (arrowed).

firmly in place, attach the stem to the stake in two places – at about 2ft(60cm) and 4ft(1.2m) above the ground. Use proprietary ties with a spacer to prevent the stakes from chafing the bark (see Fig 70).

For multi-stemmed conifers like Chamaecyparis and Taxus, or tree heathers, tie each of the main stems individually to the stake. Use soft but strong twine.

Some authorities favour using a shorter stake with a single tie at about 2½ft(75cm) above ground. Apart from being less expensive, the theory is that the extra movement of the top growth encourages firmer rooting. This may well be the case with some deciduous trees in sheltered gardens. However, recent experiences with evergreens in exposed gardens, indicate that the extra movement in winter is bad and slows down establishment, and there is an increased risk of stems snapping off. Older, harder wood low down is more brittle and less flexible than younger growth higher up the tree, and a longer stake plus at least two ties are needed for adequate support.

PLANTING IN CONTAINERS

When planting in containers, there are two main points to watch. Firstly, plants should be provided with a good growing environment and, secondly they must also look attractive when used for display. Guidelines for arranging and displaying plants for effect are discussed in Chapter 1 but never forget that it is just as important, and perhaps even more so, to match a plant's needs to site when growing in containers as when planting direct.

When dealing with newly bought in plants, the best times for setting them out in containers are spring and autumn. And, as with planting *in situ* aim to tackle the job during calm, dull, mild, showery weather.

Established, container-grown plants are potted on if they have not yet reached maturity and further growth is to be encouraged. Think in terms

Fig 72 Picea mariana 'Nana' – a compact, tight, bun-forming dwarf. Good for containers or the risk garden.

of annual potting on for quick-growing varieties and young stock. With dwarf and slow-growing conifers a move in alternate years is more the norm. Do not be too rigid, and be guided in part at least by the amount of top growth. Where the spread or height of the branches is equivalent to three times or more the width or height of the container a move is called for. Roots growing out of the bottom of the container and into the ground provide another indication that potting on would be beneficial. Spring is the best time but it is also acceptable to pot on in autumn.

Where the aim is to limit plant size and growth to existing dimensions then annual or biennial repotting into the same sized container is the norm. Limit repotting to spring.

Make sure that the plants are well-watered and tidied up, as for planting *in situ*. Check all pots and containers are clean and in good repair. Containers which are being re-used should be brushed clean of old roots and compost prior to washing and disinfecting. Allow any fumes to disperse before filling. For new containers, make sure that any fumes from timber preservatives have dissipated. Always soak concrete, simulated

Fig 71 Juniperus communis 'Compressa'. An ideal, reliable dwarf conifer which is thoroughly hardy. Well suited to container growing and to the rock garden.

65

stone and terracotta in clean water for twenty-four hours before filling. This washes away injurious salts and charges the container up with moisture. In hard water areas, use rainwater for soaking.

Cover the drainage holes in the base of containers with squares of fine mesh netting, wired into position. This serves a dual role as it prevents wash-out of potting compost and blocks the entry of worms, pests and insects. Drop in a layer of fine non-alkaline gravel or broken pieces of polystyrene to provide good drainage.

Where containers such as windowboxes, patio troughs and planters are to be used for plunge planting of smaller individual plants part fill them with peat or pulverized bark in readiness to receive the plants. Arrange the plants, complete with pots, on the bark or peat base and then pack more bark or peat round the pots right up to their rims. The rims should stand about 1in(3cm) below the top of the main container. Where liners are used to house the plunge-planted pots, the outer holder should also be bottomed out with drainage material (see Fig 73).

When moving plants on into a larger container proceed as follows:

1. Select a suitably sized container. The normal practice is to move on plants two sizes up. A plant in a 5in(1-litre) pot is moved into a 7in(3-litre) pot, and then into a 9in(5-litre) pot.
2. Net over the drainage holes and bottom out with drainage material as before. part fill with soil-based potting compost, using a lime-free mixture for heathers and other lime haters.
3. Remove the plant from its pot, loosen the roots slightly and ease out old drainage material from the base. Cut back cleanly any dead, damaged or diseased roots to sound tissue.
4. Position the plant centrally in the larger container. Work more potting compost around the sides of the rootball and firm. Cover the top of the rootball with about ½in(1cm) of potting compost. Always aim to leave a ¾–1in(2–3cm) space at the top for watering.
5. Water in and stand in a sheltered spot.

When repotting a plant into the same sized container, prepare the container as for potting on. Remove the plant from its existing container.

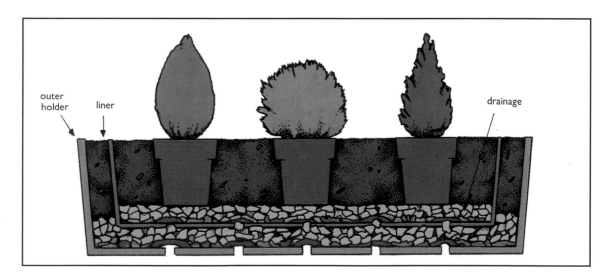

Fig 73 Plunge planting in containers – plants plunged in an interchangeable liner are being lowered into an outer holder.

Scrape the top ½in(1cm) of old compost from the top of the rootball. Poke out old compost from the base removing old drainage materials at the same time. Draw out the roots and trim back, aiming to remove up to 1in(3cm) off the bottom of the rootball depending on the size of the plant. Next tease out some of the old compost around the sides of the rootball and where roots are excessively long, shorten back slightly. Repot, working fresh potting compost around and over the rootball, again leaving a space at the top for watering. Water in, keep sheltered and shaded from strong sun until growing away again.

MULCHING

Traditionally, a mulch is a layer of bulky organic matter, such as well-rotted garden compost, leaf mould or manure. It is spread on the surface of the soil, around plants, mainly in spring. For autumn mulches see page 34.

One of the main reasons for mulching is to keep plant roots moist during summer. Towards this end, bulky organics work in two ways. Firstly, they reduce surface water evaporation during warm, dry weather and so help moisture retention. Secondly, during wet weather, they absorb surplus water and hold it in reserve for the future benefit of plants. By so doing they also halt any undue washing out of soil nutrients.

Mulches suppress weed growth so cutting down on the work involved in, and the damage done by, hoeing off weeds. Many plants resent root disturbance during the growing season and even light cultivation can be damaging to shallow rooting plants like conifers, rhododendrons and heathers — mulch and do away with the need for summer cultivations. In addition to protecting surface roots from physical damage, a mulch will also minimize any tendency to overheat under fierce summer sun.

Mulching prevents soil crusting and its subsequent adverse effect on plant growth. This is a problem found on unmulched soil as the season wears on because of the natural action of rain beating down on the soil surface. Expect crusting to be particularly bad where plants are subjected to constant watering from cans and hoses during a dry season.

Well-rotted garden composts, leaf moulds and manures are the traditional mulches providing a certain amount of nutrients as well as mulch. Never apply fresh manure as a mulch — allow it to rot first or you will risk scorch.

Without doubt, peat is the best mulch to use on lime-hating plants. However, there are a few snags and it needs careful handling. If allowed to dry out it is very difficult to re-wet. It is expensive and adds nothing in the way of nutrients.

Although mushroom compost can be useful, unless an accurate analysis can be provided, it is not recommended for a heather and conifer garden. Some samples contain an appreciable amount of lime.

Present-day proprietary bark mulches come in a variety of grades and are excellent. Be guided by your local garden centres.

Be wary about using the likes of raw grass clippings for mulching. They are best composted first to overcome weed and slime problems. Never use grass clippings from lawns recently treated with weedkillers.

Perforated mulching polythene is ideal for anyone short of organic mulches. It is a useful product in its own right for retaining moisture and retarding weed growth. For heather and conifer gardens it has, however, less practical application for heathers than conifers. Use as the makers direct. Cover the plastic with non-alkaline chippings to improve the appearance. Bait slugs and woodlice — they thrive in the moist, dark conditions under the plastic.

Give any newly planted stock priority for mulches. Established, healthy stock are better able to cope without. The timing of an application is critical. Put the mulch on before the soil dries out too much — mulches must be applied to moist soils if they are to be effective. Do not mulch too early in the season — aim to let things warm up a bit first otherwise soil temperatures will be depressed and growth delayed.

67

Fig 74 Juniperus horizontalis *'Blue Chip' – a widely grown, popular, ground-hugging, weed-smothering conifer.*

Broadly speaking, mulching should follow along these lines:

1. Hoe off the weeds.
2. Dress with fertilizer. A small handful of general fertilizer per sq yd(m) makes an average dressing. For heathers and newly-planted stock, omit the fertilizer or risk lanky, disease-prone plants and an over-abundance of foliage at the expense of flowers, and a shortened lifespan.
3. Water in the fertilizer and apply the mulch. Do not allow it to rest against the plant stems. In permanent borders, it is best to cover the whole area. If this is not possible, concentrate the mulch in deepish layers, not exceeding 2in(5cm), around individual plants. When liquid feeding conifers during summer, ease up the mulch to give improved penetration. Try to keep the mulch replenished throughout the growing season and lightly fork in any remains during autumn. The mulch will then act as a soil conditioner.

Bark mulches are not dug in during autumn. They can be left well alone or they can be topped up. Either way any remains are pulled back in spring. This is to enable the soil to warm up naturally and quickly. The bark is then replaced and replenished as need be.

WEED CONTROL

For heathers and conifers, the secret of success is to keep new plantings completely weed-free. Embark on a programme of regular hand-weeding and generous mulching for a two- or three-year period. Make hand-weeding a top priority during this initial post-planting period particularly where mulching materials are in short supply. Within a few years, you may expect ground cover heathers and conifers largely to smother out seedling weeds in beds and borders.

CHAPTER 5

Summer Scene

Summer is one of the best times of the year to see and enjoy a well-managed, representative selection of heathers and conifers. But it is also a time when newly set out plants, along with those in containers, soon suffer if watering is neglected.

It is a known fact that once established in congenial surroundings conifers, heathers and their allies demand less attention than many other garden plants. However, having said that, they will amply repay a bit of meaningful and timely care. This applies as much in summer as at any other time of year.

SUMMER CALENDAR

Many of the jobs started in spring continue on into, and even throughout, summer. A general checklist of the most important things which need attention has been drawn up as a ready reference. Adapt it to suit individual circumstances, with special regard to the age, variety and condition of the plants in question.

1.   Water and syringe over plants as necessary.
2.   Complete any unfinished spring mulching and topdressing. Where materials are available, replenish mulches throughout the season.
3.   Hoe and weed, or lightly cultivate, round any unmulched plants in beds and borders. Aim to create a dust mulch of finely broken-down soil at the surface. Dust mulches help to conserve moisture and prevent harmful surface crusting.
4.   Hand-weed under, and around, heathers and conifers.
5.   Dead-head and clip over spring flowering heathers.

6.   Cut conifer hedges. Clip topiary and shorten back any scorched or damaged growths.
7.   Set about routine and remedial pruning as required.
8.   Thin out overhanging conifers and other evergreens to let in light and air to underplantings of sun-loving heathers and variegated conifers.
9.   Continue to remove suckers from grafted conifers and cut out any reverted green shoots from variegated varieties.
10.   Liquid feed conifers where they missed dry spring fertilizer dressings.
11.   Adjust and replace supports and ties as the need arises.
12.   Take the opportunities, as they arise, to push ahead with new works and improvements including site clearance, levelling, drainage and pre-planting cultivations. A good time to construct new features like rocky mounds, peat pockets, raised beds, plunge beds.
13.   Take cuttings of heathers and heather allies.
14.   Liquid feed container-grown conifers.
15.   Protect recently potted plants from wind and strong sun until re-established.
16.   Water plants regularly — daily in warm, dry weather and syringe over if need be.

WATERING

Incorrect watering is one of the most common underlying causes of plant malaise.

Overwatering leads to waterlogging of the rooting medium. This in turn results in the suffocation and drowning of the roots and the consequential death of the plant in extreme cases. Excessive watering also results in undue washing

Fig 75 Erica cinerea *'Pink Ice' – a summer flowering acid-loving variety which stands dry conditions better than most.*

out of soluble plant nutrients and unless replenished, plants soon suffer from starvation. Starvation is most immediately noticeable in plants with the type of restricted root run typical of container growing.

Lack of moisture and dryness of the roots or foliage affects plants in a variety of ways depending on the severity of the dryness:

1. It limits the uptake of essential nutrients from the soil because these must be absorbed in solution.
2. It slows down, or halts, the manufacture of starches and sugars within the plant. As a consequence, growth is poor.

3. It causes overheating of the plant, and wilting and scorching of leaves during periods of strong sunlight. As water becomes scarce, the cooling effect of moisture evaporation from leaves and soil is virtually wiped out.

When to Water

To risk stating the obvious, the need to water is most acute when natural rainfall is insufficient to replenish soil moisture and sustain growth. For heathers and conifers only water when absolutely necessary or risk the roots becoming lazy and inefficient. You should however water:

1. Plants of any age which are growing in containers and beginning to dry out. Never let them dry to a critical level.
2. Immediately before and after potting or transplanting.
3. In drying weather conditions especially fierce sun and wind.
4. Plants in free-draining soils. Pay particular attention to young plants and any others which have recently been moved but are not yet fully established. It takes one or two seasons for a plant to become fully established and cope with adverse conditions.
5. Established conifers which have been root pruned in readiness for moving into new positions, or where they have been moved and are not yet re-established.
6. Before mulching in spring – this is vital when dry feeding.
7. Before any plant is in danger of drying out to a critical degree no matter where they are growing. Late spring and summer are the most vulnerable times.

Knowing fairly precisely the frequency of when to water comes as second nature given a few years of keen observation, practice and experience. Newcomers to the scene may have problems with the frequency of watering until they get the feel of it.

One fairly simple rule of thumb guide with

plants set out in the ground is to water newly planted stock about twice or three times weekly during sunny, dry weather in late spring and summer. Once or twice weekly will normally suffice in dull but dry weather.

Container plants will need watering daily in hot, dry, sunny weather and twice a day in extreme conditions. Think in terms of three or four times weekly in dull but dry weather.

Regardless of guidelines, get into the habit of testing the soil or potting compost for dryness. Simply disturb the soil and feel down about 1in(3cm) below the surface. If dry, then water. For the newcomer, wishing for a bit more accuracy, a soil moisture meter can help until experience is gained. But this can really only be justified where quite a number of valuable plants are involved.

To minimize the risk of scorch caused by the magnifying-glass effect of water droplets on foliage, do not water plants in strong sun.

Watering Techniques and Water Quality

Having decided that watering is necessary, it then remains to decide how best to apply the water and how much to give.

In hard water districts where the mains water supply is lime-rich, water composition is of particular importance when growing heathers and heather allies. Do not be tempted to use the lime-rich mains water unless for short periods in time of emergency. And never use water which has been treated with water softener. Wherever practical, collect and use rainwater.

Container plants are normally watered from the top until drainage water starts to trickle out from the bottom. With well-managed plants, this is usually indicative of a sufficiency of moisture but do ensure that water is not merely running down between rootball and the sides of the container. This can all too often happen where the compost has been allowed to dry out. In these circumstances, pack moist potting compost to in-fill the space. Then water slowly and persistently to re-wet.

When watering direct-planted stock it is very important to apply enough water at any one time to ensure thorough percolation. This encourages healthy, deeper rooting, and for heathers and dwarf conifers this means applying a minimum of ½–1 gallons(2–5 litres) per watering per single plant in isolation. You should increase this to between 2–4 gallons(10–20 litres) per sq yd(m) when watering group plantings in beds and borders. Apply a similar amount to larger specimen trees and shrubs. Ball watering – soaking each rootball out to the tips of the roots rather than wetting the whole surface area – is less wasteful and more effective than overall watering. The exception to this general rule applies when watering plunge bed containers of conifers – they can be irrigated by sprinkler in the cool of the evening. Water at the same yd(m) rate of application as for group plantings above.

A watering can with rose attachment is quite adequate for watering in small gardens where only a few plants are involved. The alternative for larger areas is to use a hose with a rose or nozzle attachment.

When using a hose or sprinkler for watering, it is important to calculate the flow-through rate. It is often a great deal slower than the eye perceives. After connecting a hose, simply open up the tap a convenient number of turns, then time how long it takes to fill, say, a 2-gallon(10-litre) bucket. When gauging the rate of flow-through in a sprinkler, position a jam jar under the sprinkler. A half inch(1cm) of water in the jar represents an application rate of 2 gallons per sq yd(10 litres per sq m).

Syringing the foliage is normally reserved for container and newly transplanted conifers during hot or windy days in dry weather. It is a job for the evenings. Syringing with clean water freshens up plants. Plants can absorb an appreciable amount of water through the leaves and this is an ability which reduces stress and is of particular benefit in the case of newly set out stock where the roots are not fully established and fully functional.

FEEDING

Generally, heathers and conifers have very modest requirements when it comes to fertilizer applications. The basic nutrients involved are much the same as other garden plants but they are needed to a lesser degree. Heathers in particular suffer if overfed.

In an average garden situation, fertilizer would normally be applied in the first instance as a pre-planting dressing. For direct-planted stock, these are worked into the ground in advance of planting, and in the case of container plants, fertilizer is mixed into the potting compost before potting. Pre-planting fertilizer applications are intended to provide an initial supply of nutrients and raise fertility.

Subsequent fertilizer applications depend on plant vigour. To direct-planted stock they may be made annually, bi-annually or only occasionally. Regardless of the frequency they are normally applied in spring to beds and borders just before mulching. Plants in pockets are rather different and they are given fertilizer in the form of annual topdressings of potting compost – a treatment which is also suitable for container-grown conifers. In addition, container-grown conifers need to be given dilute liquid fertilizer during the main growing season. Apply liquid feed at 21–28 day intervals starting in spring and continuing until early August. Do not feed any later than this or risk soft, lush growth liable to frost injury in winter. Fertilizers are given to growing plants to help replenish soil nutrients which have been taken up by plants and washed out in drainage.

Materials

The present practice of using proprietary convenience feeds is sound, economical and hard to beat.

On soils of average fertility, a pre-planting dressing of bonemeal, equivalent to about one handful per sq yd(m), is worked into beds and borders. Additional fertilizer is provided in the planting mixtures used when setting out in pits and pockets. For container work, select a potting compost which comes ready made with a complete balanced fertilizer incorporated.

For post-planting fertilizers give conifers a handful of complete balanced fertilizer per sq yd(m) as required in spring. If using other proprietary fertilizers, follow the maker's instructions. For heathers, substitute a similar quantity of bonemeal for the balanced fertilizer. It is slower and gentler and is better suited to heathers than the more soluble, quicker acting proprietary mixtures. When using liquid fertilizer, be sure to use a complete balanced potash tomato-type liquid feed, and always make it up as per the instructions.

PRUNING AND CLIPPING

Broadly speaking, when compared to many other garden trees and shrubs, heathers and conifers need less pruning. When pruning aim:

1. To achieve and then maintain good health and optimum vigour.
2. To shape up plants and then keep them looking good.
3. To ensure free and continued flowering in the case of heathers and their allies.

Success with pruning and clipping depends on three major factors: timing, cutting and aftercare.

Timing can be critical. Heathers are normally cut over as soon as possible after flowering. Dead flowers are removed promptly to prevent seed production and its resultant weakening effect on plants. By clipping immediately after flowering, plants are also afforded the maximum length of time to build up their energy reserves before flowering comes round again. Do not cut or clip conifers during winter or when the foliage is frozen. The danger is scorch and stem splitting. The ideal time to deal with conifers is late spring and summer. Always cut out dead, dying or badly diseased growths at the earliest opportunity.

*Fig 76 When pruning, always cut cleanly back
to a good bud, or a main stem, or to a
healthy shoot as here.*

*Fig 77 Shorten overlong, damaged or straggly
shoots and roots before planting.*

For correct cutting make sure that pruners and shears are clean, well lubricated and sharp. The important point here is that all cuts must be made cleanly with a complete absence of jagged and torn edges. Make the cut close to a prominent bud or vigorous secondary growth (see Fig 76). Larger growths are usually taken back to a main branch. When cutting out dead or diseased wood, always shorten back to sound, healthy tissue.

As soon as pruning and clipping are finished for the day, clean up and dispose of the remains. Whenever wounds of ¾in(2cm) and over in diameter are made, take steps to reduce the risk of entry of disease and undue loss of sap. This is done by paring with a sharp knife to smooth over the saw cuts and then painting with a suitable proprietary sealant.

Simple Pruning

Try to think of pruning in stages, taking into account the age and condition of the shrubs or trees in question. First, formation pruning involves pruning and training of young plants into the required shape. For heathers and conifers this is minimal. Next is routine pruning, and there are also the advantages of remedial and renovation pruning to consider. This aspect of pruning is mainly concerned with the corrective pruning and treatment of old, damaged or diseased trees and shrubs (see page 81).

When planting heathers, shorten back any straggly or damaged shoots and, and having gently spread out the roots, shorten back any that are diseased, damaged or overlong.

Subsequently, heathers are pruned or clipped annually. Summer and autumn flowering varieties are normally best pruned as soon as flowering is over with foliage varieties being the exception. They may be left until spring. This delayed pruning allows them to give a greater display of winter colour. Remove the flowered spikes and clusters when pruning and clipping but leave the basal foliage largely untouched apart from shortening back overlong or straggly growths.

Dwarf winter and spring flowering heathers are ideally trimmed as soon as the flowers fade –

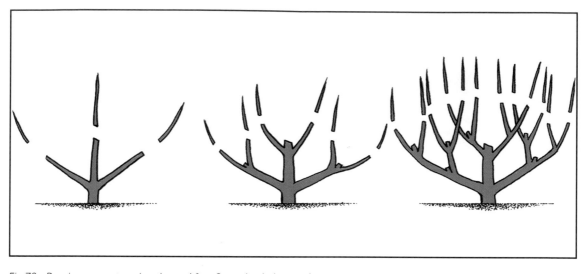

Fig 78 Pruning young tree heathers. After flowering in late spring, shorten the previous season's new growth by half. Left to right – in the first, second and third years.

not even waiting until they are dead. This is to create maximum time for new growth. Foliage varieties are treated no differently to the other kinds. The actual pruning technique is as for summer and autumn flowering kinds.

When pruning tree heathers shorten the main leading growths back by about half their length as the flowers fade for the first four years. This encourages the development of bushy, basal growths. Subsequently, clip off the flower heads as blooming ceases.

Heather allies need little or no regular pruning apart from shortening back and removing old, outworn, dead or diseased stems. *Phyllodoce* is an exception, and it is treated in very much the same way as spring flowering heathers.

At planting time conifers should be shortened back to remove untidy, straggly, damaged or diseased shoots and roots. Subsequent treatment depends very much on how the conifers are to be treated – are they to be grown in natural style or clipped?

For a natural, free-form style minimal pruning is required. Prune to shape and remove any damaged growths – best carried out in late spring or summer. Shorten back untidy, over-

long, damaged or misplaced shoots, and shorten or cut out any dead or diseased wood. Varieties grown as trees are usually limited to a single main stem.

For clipped conifers, and hedging in particular, allow the plants to reach their intended height before cutting out the main growing leader, or leaders, at the top. However, in the interim, do not neglect to cut in at the sides at least once or twice each summer. This encourages a thick, dense, bushy texture. Whenever 4–6in(10–15cm) of side growth is made, shorten this back by one third to a half, and this is another job best tackled during late spring or summer. When clipping hedges and specimen conifers it is important to make sure that the sides slope inwards, so leaving the base wider than the top. This helps to ensure that the lower branches are not robbed of light. If lower branches are too shaded, loss of foliage and consequential bare stems are the inevitable results.

Low growing and prostrate ground cover conifers are clipped over the tops and around the edges as necessary during summer, more or less from the time they are planted out, in order to restrict them to their allotted space.

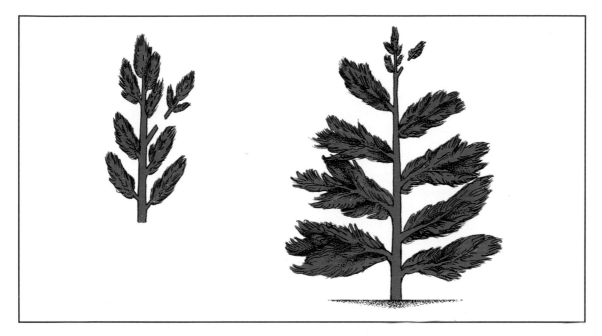

Fig 79   When forking on a single stem tree conifer occurs, leave one main
stem and cut out any secondary, inferior or less well-placed leaders.

Fig 80   Clip only the sides of a conifer hedge until the required height is
reached, when the top should also be cut. Keep the top narrower than
the base.

Training Topiary

Yew is really the only conifer suited to topiary training and it ranks with the very best shrubs for the purpose. When clipped, its dense texture is second to none. Yews can also be grown in containers for topiary training – think in terms of a 12in(30cm) minimum sized container for a mature yew topiary.

Select a healthy young plant which branches from the base, and, most importantly, is well foliaged from the bottom up. Whatever the intended shape, give the shrub a bit of extra cossetting. This is to promote the sought-after steady, compact growth needed to form a solid, bushy shrub. Clip when the shoots are young and clip lightly and clip regularly though, as with any other evergreen, confine clipping to late spring and summer and always leave the shrub wider at the base than the top, and never cut back into old wood.

To create the basic shapes of a simple pyramid, cone, ball or cube you need little other than a good eye, a steady hand and a willingness to clip regularly. Once the required height and shape has been achieved, it is vital to continue clipping regularly to keep the shrub healthy and in trim. Allow five to seven years for a simple topiary to reach fruition and double this time for anything more elaborate.

The double ball or poodle is a popular topiary for beginners. Train the yew into a ball leaving two or three strong central shoots to grow up. Encourage them to make strong growth until they reach about 2ft(60cm) above the first ball. Strip off the foliage immediately above the first ball to create a 12in(30cm) length of bare stems – in effect separating the first ball from the second. Then set about training the topmost 12in(30cm) into a second ball. It is quite feasible to go on and create a third ball in a similar manner.

Where a hedge is broken by a gateway try creating a connecting arch. A wire arch supporting frame will be needed and they are available

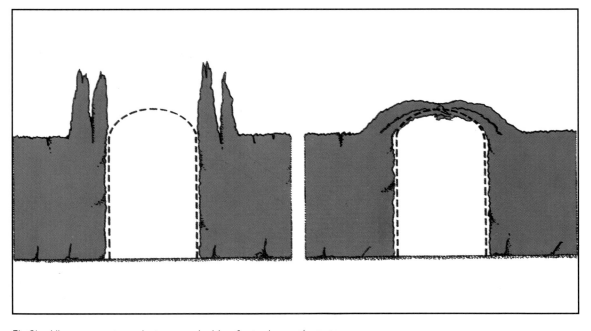

Fig 81   Allow one or two plants on each side of a topiary archway to grow unchecked upwards. Train them over a wire frame. Bend over when long enough to meet, and tie down.

through garden centres. Having positioned the arch, allow some strong shoots to grow up either side. Tie in the shoots neatly and regularly and clip as they grow. When they meet at the top, encourage them to grow into each other to create a dense, overhead canopy. Given time, yew makes a first class archway.

Birds, animals and more elaborate shapes are best reserved for the experienced. Training is generally onto supporting frames which must be strong and constructed of stout wire to give a simple, well-proportioned outline on which to build. It takes a modicum of skill and ingenuity to achieve the desired effect. Position the frame, part the shoots low down, divide them out and tie them in. Eventually they will cover all sides of the frame. It is imperative that they are tied in frequently and clipped regularly as they grow. For filling up in case of trouble, keep a few cutting-raised plants growing on elsewhere in the garden.

PLANT PROTECTION

The protection of plants from the excesses of wind, weather and other afflictions like pests and diseases does not always receive the attention it deserves. The ideal is to strike a happy balance and not becoming obsessed or pre-occupied with notions of overprotection. Many problems are avoidable in the first place given good planning and layout, a careful choice of plants, thorough site preparations and the adoption of sound planting practices.

Many varieties of heathers and conifers are reliably hardy and do not need a lot of nursing or fuss especially once established. Plants most at risk are those in containers, and those newly set out which are not yet fully established. The main weather factors to guard against are wind and sun, frost and snow, excessive shade and wet.

Wind

Wind is directly responsible for many forms of plant damage – breakage, drying out, foliage and

Fig 82 Hybrid larch – an extremely hardy light textured tree which is suitable for exposed gardens where space allows.

flower scorch, chilling, wind pruning and loosening of plant roots. Plants are weakened, growth is retarded and, in severe cases, the plant may die. Freezing cold and drying winds from the north and east can be particularly damaging to many conifers in winter and spring. Heathers are generally better adapted to withstand strong winds than conifers.

The main objective of gardeners combating wind in exposed gardens should be to reduce the wind force coming into contact with valued plants – particularly anything newly set out. It is a well-known fact that, as a rule, wind damage worsens as wind speed increases. Permeable windscreens, which allow the air to filter

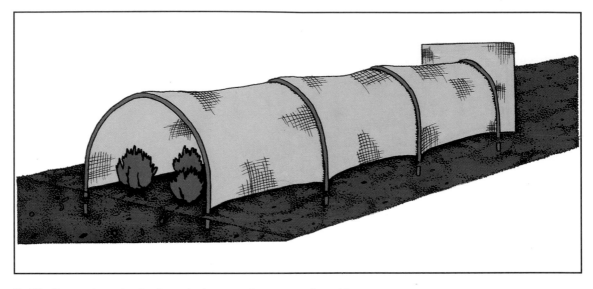

Fig 83   Fine mesh netting fixed to wire hoops to form a tunnel provides a safe haven for young plants, provided it is sealed at both ends with netting. Fresh air and water can pass through but shelter from strong sun and high wind is assured.

through, are much more effective than solid walls or fences which can cause damaging wind turbulence in high winds.

In the short term, temporary windscreens of fine mesh netting, having somewhere in the region of 50 per cent permeability and fixed to a supporting framework, are effective both for single plants and for groups. Provide protection on three sides and back the screen into the direction of the prevailing wind.

The height of any windscreen should be sufficient to protect the tops as well as the lower parts of plants. With this in mind, remember that, on level ground, a screen across the direction of the wind will only give protection for a distance equal to about four times its height. A 6ft(1.8m) high screen will shelter a strip of ground up to 24ft(7m) wide. Trellis screens placed across the ends of gaps between buildings will provide reasonable shelter in these notoriously windy and draughty locations. Netting tunnels, on low structures with the ends sealed, give good shelter for such as tender ground cover plants in exposed gardens, until established. They are useful too for protecting young plants. In open, windswept gardens, one long-term solution is a hedge of such as beech or hornbeam.

Sun and High Temperatures

Strong sun is mainly a problem of container-growing during spring and summer, and of newly set out plants. The effect of early morning sun on frozen flowers and foliage should not be dismissed lightly and blackening of foliage, buds and shoots are typical of the damage in these situations.

The remedy in most cases where fierce and early morning sun threatens, is to shade plants at critical times, and fine mesh netting is one of the best materials to use for the purpose. The effects of sun and high temperatures must be viewed in conjunction with moisture. Ensure that newly set out plants in particular are kept well watered.

Rainfall and Wet

Problems and remedies associated with soil drainage are considered on pages 41–2.

Frost

The influence and effects of frost on a plant's growth and well being is closely related to other factors such as wind and sun, and these should be included in any meaningful discussions on frost. Container plants are particularly at risk from frost damage.

Frost can damage plants in a variety of ways, though there are reliably hardy varieties of heathers and conifers which can tolerate intense cold. Therefore the wise choice of varieties for cold winter areas can minimize the risks of frost damage.

Frost damages newly set out plants by frost heave — lifting and exposing roots to drying winds and sun, and lifted plants must be re-firmed as soon as conditions allow, and exposed roots must be covered with fine soil or planting mix if irreparable damage is to be avoided. In cold winter areas, bark mulches applied in autumn can help.

The risk of low temperature injury can be greatly reduced by covering over with fine mesh netting in autumn. Again this is of special significance in cold winter areas and to newly set out and young plants.

Pollution

It is difficult for individuals to counter the pollution menace of fumes, soot, grime and chemicals. Conifers are more at risk than many heathers which lose at least some of their grimy foliage annually when pruning. Occasional hosing of conifers during spring and summer will help to remove surface dust and grime. Try to keep plants out of contact with car exhaust fumes, detergents from car washing, salt spray from roads, oil spillage and the like. Choose carefully when selecting plants for town gardens.

Fouling by cats and dogs

Reference has already been made (page 55) to dogs defoliating the bases of conifers by urinating on the lower foliage and the consequential need to protect plants with such as a netting barrier, especially when young.

In built-up areas with high cat populations, heathers are at risk from heavy fouling should the cats of the neighbourhood so decide. Being creatures of habit, the aim should be to discourage cats in the first place or to break the habit if once started. The use of animal deterrents can help. But a physical barrier of such as prickly, bushy twigs, pushed thickly into the ground amongst the heathers is more effective. Leave them in place for a minimum of two or three weeks. Alternatively net over the heathers for a similar length of time. Be at the ready and prepared to repeat all the preventative measures at any time.

PEST AND DISEASE CONTROL

Well-grown heathers and conifers in sympathetic surroundings usually manage to escape most problems and ailments. But neglect, extremes of weather, bad siting, poor management and careless neighbours with pest or disease-ridden plants can tip the scales to result in troubles of one sort or another.

Prevention is the best defence, and for heather and conifer growing this means good cultivation. Start with sturdy, healthy plants and give them the best possible soil and site conditions. Then with good management, timely attention to detail and strict hygiene, many sources of potential trouble are automatically eliminated.

However, even in the best regulated gardens troubles can strike at almost any time. In an effort to put things right there are three main techniques which can be adopted:

1. *Sanitation pruning* Cut out dead or badly infected growths in an effort to eliminate sources of infection.
2. *Protective chemicals* One or more of their various forms, such as sprays, dusts, drenches, fumigants and paints, can be used.
3. *Errors of cultivation* These should be

79

corrected. See to such as watering, feeding, soil drainage, pruning and excessive shade.

Success with remedial measures depends on correct diagnosis followed by appropriate action – nowhere more so than when using chemicals or righting faults of cultivation. There is, for example, little point in treating plants against insect pests when the real trouble is a fungus disease. When using chemicals, follow the makers' directions to the letter. Read the small print carefully both in the interests of safety and successful treatment.

The following are some of the ailments most likely to be met. For details of susceptibilities, *see* individual entries in Chapter 7.

Pests

Adelges These gall-forming insects are conspicuous on conifers by the presence of small pineapple-like galls on the shoots, or by white woolly tufts on the foliage. The foliage soon becomes brownish and discoloured. Expect stunted growth in the case of affected plants.
Treatment Pick or cut off affected shoots and dispose of the remains. Spray affected plants with an approved insecticide in spring.

Aphids (various) These greenish or yellowish-green insects usually congregate in colonies at or near the growing point causing distorted and stunted growth. Aphid attack is normally accompanied by honeydew – a shiny, sticky fluid. Sometimes, black, sooty moulds develop on the honeydew creating unsightly patches.
Treatment Spray affected plants with a suitable insecticide, such as one based on malathion.

Caterpillars (various) Grubs of different size, shape and colour can attack to devour the foliage. Some may conceal themselves in rolls of foliage or in web-like tents.
Treatment In small-scale attacks hand-pick the caterpillars. The alternative is to spray with an insecticide such as one based on derris.

Red Spider Mite *(Panonychus)* In severe attacks – and attacks have usually become severe before they are discernible by a casual glance – the foliage becomes dull green or bronzed and there is evidence of fine webbing together with numerous red or yellowish red mites. These normally seek the shelter of leaf undersides. Plants near dry walls are the most vulnerable.
Treatment Hot, dry days favour this pest – spray over the foliage in the evening. Treat with insecticide such as derris or malathion paying attention to wetting the leaf undersides.

Diseases and Disorders

Chlorosis This is a non-infectious disorder resulting in yellowing of the foliage and stunted growth. It occurs mainly among lime-hating plants when they are grown on alkaline soils.
Treatment Avoid growing lime haters in alkaline soils. Grow them in containers or rocky peaty pockets of lime-free potting compost or planting mixture. And always use rainwater for irrigation in hard water areas. Drench the roots of affected plants with iron sequestrene.

Damping off (various) This is a fungus disease which attacks young seedlings at soil level causing them to topple over and die. There is no effective cure.
Treatment Prevention is the only answer. Use clean containers and disease-free fresh compost for sowing seeds. Avoid high temperatures and over-wet compost during germination. If watering is needed, always water seed trays from below by standing in a container of clean water. Where there have been problems in the past, before watering add just sufficient potassium permanganate to the water to turn it pink.

Dieback (various) Progressive dying back is usually caused by disease organisms attacking the tips but it may be due to root or stem rots or to poor soil conditions. This results in dying back of branches, shoots and foliage from the tips back towards the main crown or head.

Treatment Cut off dead tips back to sound growth and spray with a good fungicide such as Bordeaux Mixture or other proprietary copper preparation. Dig out any dead or dying plants. Improve drainage if it is suspect.

Heather wilt (various) The symptoms are similar to dieback. There is a characteristic greying and dying of shoot tips and sometimes whole plants are killed. The cause is usually fungus attack.
Treatment As for dieback.

Honeyfungus *(Armillaria)* Where the wilting of unthrifty plants worsens progressively look for signs of honey-coloured toadstools. These are typical of honeyfungus and arise from the base of dead or diseased plants. Another sign is the appearance of dark brown bootlace-like rhizoides just below the soil surface spreading out from diseased plants. Once infected, plants are usually killed in time.
Treatment There is no cure. Dig out and burn dead plants complete with the bootlaces. Disinfect affected soil with cresylic acid type preparation, allowing fumes to disperse before replanting.

Stem and trunk rot (various) The starting point of trunk and stem rots is usually injury, insect damage or unfavourable soil conditions such as water lodging around the base of the stem or trunk.
Treatment Where practical, cut out damaged or rotting pieces of stem back to sound wood. Paint over wounds with a suitable safe horticultural sealant.

Thuja leaf blight *(Keithia)* A disease of *Thuja* varieties. Typical symptoms include blackening and browning of the foliage leaving bare stems.
Treatment Spray over affected plants promptly, at the first signs of attack using a good fungicide such as Bordeaux Mixture. Repeat again in fourteen days and thereafter as necessary. Avoid overcrowding plants.

RENOVATION OF CONIFERS

Many conifers can be rejuvenated and have their lifespan extended by remedial pruning. This is more demanding and requires greater expertise than routine pruning, and before attempting any tree work which cannot be easily managed from ground level, do weigh up the problems involved, and obtain professional advice if in any doubt. Most remedial pruning is of special significance to old and neglected plants.

Old conifers, notably *Cedrus* and *Pinus*, often benefit from having a few of the lowest, outworn branches removed. This not only tidies them up and removes possible sources of disease but also effectively gives more headroom under the trees for such as bulbs and ground cover. The ideal time to carry out the work is summer. Small branches up to about 1½in(4cm) thick are cut off flush with the trunk. Thicker and larger limbs are best removed in manageable sections by lopping.

Fig 84 The removal of lower branches may be carried out (crown raising) when they have served their useful purpose and/or when extra headroom is needed for underplanting. Cut off large branches in sections and finish flush with the main stem. Paint over wounds with sealing compound.

81

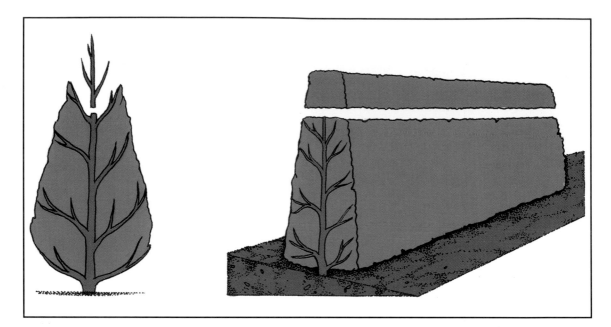

Fig 85   When lowering a tree or hedge, do not remove more than one
third in a year or you will risk dieback or death.

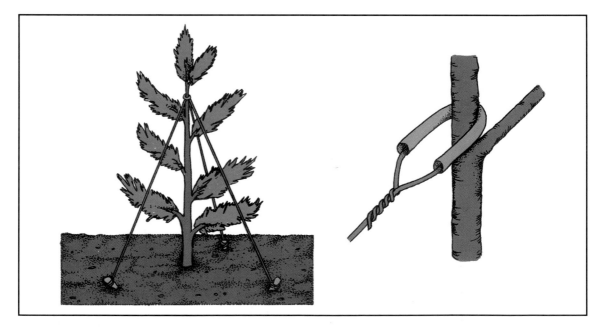

Fig 86   Guying is a useful method of supporting unstable young trees.
Attach three wires to the main stem and securely fix to pegs evenly
spaced around the base, pulling the wires taut. To avoid chafing the bark,
pass each wire through a piece of soft hosepipe.

82

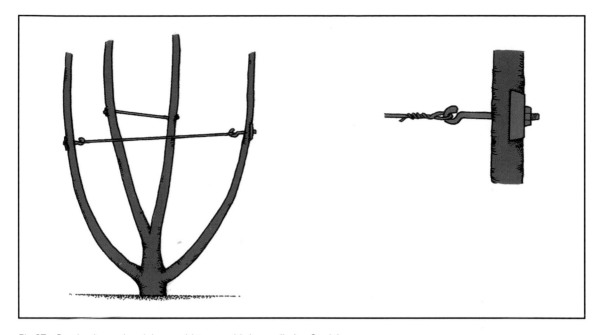

Fig 87 Bracing is used mainly on old trees with heavy limbs. Straining wires are attached to eyelets, using the weight of one limb to counterbalance another. A job best left to experts.

The selective thinning out of whole branches to let in light and air is sometimes necessary and practical with trees of open spreading habit like some *Cedrus* and *Araucaria*. Lop the branches, removing up to, but no more than, one third their total number. Again always paint over sawcuts with sealant. This is a job best left to tree surgeons for any specimen over about 12ft(3.5m) in height.

Curbing the skyward tendency of plants is a very common problem. It is normally safe to remove up to the top third of the height of a conifer provided the work is carried out in late spring or summer. Smooth over any sawcuts with a sharp knife and paint over wounds with a safe horticultural sealant.

Sometimes it is feasible to support unstable, relatively young, healthy vigorous conifers up to about 12ft(3.5m) in height until they re-establish. Those which have been loosened by high winds or falling trees come into this category. It may be noted that any old large and unstable tree is a hazard, especially near property, paths and traffic, and is best taken down. Do not attempt to support as new root growth is unlikely.

In many instances, the single stake method of support is not practical and this is where the technique of guying becomes a possibility. Guying consists of looping three wires around the main stem, about two thirds up the tree, and fixing these to pegs in the ground. It is normal to hammer home three pegs securely into the ground. Space them at equal distances, about 3ft(90cm) out from, and around, the base of the conifer. Ensure they are positioned where they are least likely to get in the way. Protect the main stem by passing each wire through a length of plastic or rubber hose-pipe which prevents bare wires rubbing the stem. The wires are gently pulled, evenly taut, and each secured to a peg. Future adjustments of the wires is relatively a simple matter.

Sometimes the branches of old, multi-stem *Taxus* and *Chamaecyparis* tend to be forced apart under the weight of snow, heavy driving rain or wind. This can be prevented by bracing/tying in the branches about half to two thirds of the way up. Use inconspicuous plastic coated wire for the purpose. Again, when dealing with large or heavy limbed trees over, say, 15ft(4.5m) in height, it is advisable to get qualified, on-the-spot advice.

CHAPTER 6

Simple Propagation

PROPAGATING TECHNIQUES

The vast majority of home-raised heathers and conifers are propagated from cuttings, divisions, layers and seeds. Grafting is generally reserved for the more experienced and is used a lot in the trade to increase some of the more fickle varieties of conifers.

The choice of method is governed by factors such as plant variety, season and the use for which the plants are ultimately intended. One extremely important point to accept at the outset is the essential difference between using seed and propagating clonally from such as cuttings and layers. Seed-raised stock are variable while those raised clonally are identical to their parents.

The majority of gardenworthy heathers and conifers need to be propagated clonally. Only then can it be guaranteed that the young plants are identical to the parent stock. Seed-raised progeny frequently look quite different from their parents and from each other within a batch. It is because of this that the main use of seed is for the production of conifer rootstocks in readiness for grafting.

Division

Division should only be regarded as a practical proposition when dealing with low growing, creeping or thicket-forming heathers and heather allies. It involves detaching rooted segments from donor (parent) plants and represents a fairly natural means of increase.

Autumn, or mild spells in early winter, are the best times to tackle plant division. Using a hand fork, carefully tease the soil away from around selected plants to expose the rooted segments. Detach the outermost and most vigorous of these disturbing the parent as little as possible. Ensure neither parent nor division dries out, and with this in mind, promptly pack lime-free potting compost or peaty topsoil to infill the cavity created by the removal of the division and water in thoroughly. Similarly pot up the young divisions into lime-free ericaceous potting mixture without delay, and again water freely to settle the compost in and around the roots. Move the pots under cover to provide immediate protection from wind and weather. A garden frame or a ventilated propagating box is ideal for the purpose.

Layering

Layering is a method of propagation which has proved highly successful and popular with many heather enthusiasts. However, it is not confined exclusively to heathers and heather allies. A number of conifers can also be increased by using variations of the layering technique. With layering there are two points of particular appeal. First is the high success rate — 90 per cent plus is possible. And secondly, a minimum of equipment is required.

The best times for layering are autumn or spring. Select longish shoots, of one or two year's growth and within easy reach of soil level. Then make a shallow furrow about 1½in(4cm) deep and about 3in(8cm) long, in line with the shoot. Bottom out the furrow with lime-free potting compost for heathers and heather allies. Use standard potting compost for conifers. Using a

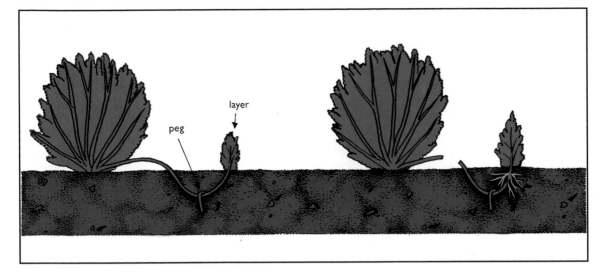

Fig 88 *Young heather shoots are pegged down into prepared soil with tips vertical. When the layer is rooted sever the stem connecting parent and progeny. Leave for about 21 days before lifting.*

piece of bent wire, peg the shoot down securely into the furrow at a point about 3in(8cm) from the tip. Cover the stem with more potting compost so as to form a small mound over the wire pin. Make the mound about 1in(3cm) higher than the level of the surrounding soil. Keep the tip of

Fig 89 *Carefully detach well-rooted outer segments and pot up in potting compost. Grow on under cover until established.*

the layer as near to the vertical as possible when mounding and, where practical, tie it to a cane pushed firmly into the ground. Subsequently, keep the pegged down layer moist – this is particularly important during the first spring and summer. For heathers and their allies, water with rainwater whenever possible.

Within about twelve months the layers of heathers and their allies should be well rooted and the connecting stem between layer and parent can be severed in safety. Expect conifers to take longer. The majority need two years and longer to form a good root system. After severance it is important to leave layers for a month to six weeks before lifting and planting out. In all but the mildest areas it is preferable to plant out the young layered plants in spring. Autumn planting is as reliably successful as spring in favoured gardens in mild districts.

Cuttings

Heather and conifer enthusiasts are concerned in the main with the taking and preparation of cuttings of a semi-ripewood nature.

Heather cuttings are usually taken sometime between May and July. The condition of the shoot is more important than the calendar date.

Fig 90 Left: a tip cutting of heather. Right: a
conifer cutting. Both taken with heels and
prepared ready for insertion in pots of cutting
compost.

1. Bottom out the pots with a 1in(3cm) layer of acid grit for drainage.
2. Top up with a 50:50 peat:acid grit mixture and level off the top.
3. Insert the prepared cuttings about ¾in(2cm) apart and about ½in(1cm) deep.
4. Water from above, using a can with a fine rose.
5. Ideally stand the pots of cuttings inside a propagator. (A seed-tray size propagator with clear plastic cover will provide near perfect rooting conditions.)
6. Spread a 1in(3cm) deep layer of clean, fine grit or sand between and around the pots.
7. Damp over the grit/sand before replacing the plastic cover.
8. Shade the cuttings from strong sun but ensure they have good light.
9. Keep the cuttings moist until well rooted and ready to pot up singly – this usually takes about four to six weeks.

Shoots should be in a non-flowering state with a firm but green stem – avoid any which are brown, woody and hard. Select 1–1½in (3–4cm) shoots of current season's growth.

There are two recognized ways of taking heather cuttings. Young sideshoots of the right size and condition can be gently pulled down and away from the main stem, removing a piece of old stem (heel) at the same time. Alternatively, the tips of suitable sideshoots can be cut off with a sharp knife. The heel cuttings are prepared by shortening any stringy pieces of stem attached to the heel. Semi-ripewood tips should be cut cleanly to the required length of 1–1½in(3–4cm). Opinions differ about the need to leave or remove the lower leaves. From personal experience, cuttings root just as well when their leaves are left intact as when they are removed. Proprietary rooting hormones are not necessary.

All cuttings should be inserted in their rooting medium without delay. They must not be allowed to dry out at any stage. Root the cuttings in clean 3in(8cm) pots:

Cuttings from heather allies are taken in much the same way as for heathers with one or two slight variations. Firstly, the cuttings are usually longer, 1½–3in(4–8cm) being the norm, and in the case of broad-leaved varieties, the bottom two or three leaves should be removed. Allow the cuttings extra space to root, grow and develop – insert them, say, 2in(5cm) apart around the edges of small pots.

Conifer cuttings are taken with a small 'heel' and should be about 3–4in(8–10cm) in length. Leaves should be left intact. Although proprietary rooting hormone is not essential it can help to ensure a more even and quicker root development. Insert the cuttings about 2in(5cm) apart in small pots or seed trays, prepared as for heathers, using a 50:50 peat:fine grit rooting medium.

Conifer cuttings taken in September and early October root fairly readily under a garden frame or in a propagating box. Do not allow them to dry out and do give them extra protection from frost in severe weather. By about April most should be ready to pot up singly into small pots.

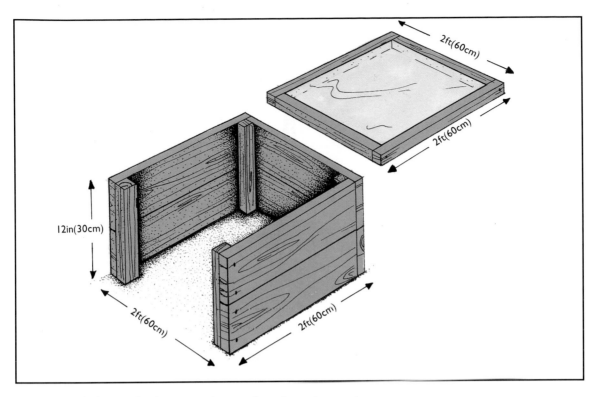

Fig 91 A simple box made of tongue and groove boarding and covered with a frame light makes a useful propagating case. ¾in(20cm) square timbers serve for corner pieces, and for making the frame light. Heavy-gauge clear plastic sheet tacked to the frame makes an inexpensive light. Paint all woodwork with exterior paint and allow fumes to disperse before use. Secure box base to pegs in the ground, and wire down the light to prevent it blowing about.

Grafting

Grafting is usually left to trained commercial propagators and is normally resorted to only when other methods fail to achieve the desired results. The theory behind grafting is to unite a piece of the required shrub with a closely related, seed-raised, actively growing, well-rooted, containerized plant (the rootstock).

There is no good reason why the keen and enthusiastic amateur should not have a go at grafting. Towards this end there are two techniques of particular note which consistently give good results, namely saddle grafting for rhododendrons and side grafting for conifers. Both are usually carried out in spring and are perhaps best described by means of illustrations (see Figs 92 and 93).

Immediately after grafting, move the plant into a well-lit spot under cover protected from drying winds and strong sun. Graft and rootstock should be united within about twenty-eight days. Once new growth is evident, harden the young plant off to acclimatize it to outdoor conditions. The easiest way is to subject plants to increased ventilation by standing in such as a garden frame or propagating box. Aim to give full ventilation day and night after about fourteen days. Grow the plants on for about two or three years.

Raising from Seed

Enthusiasts tend to ignore seed as a method of raising heathers. For conifers, growing from seed can be of interest for propagating quick-growing varieties, for producing rootstocks for grafting, for bonsai culture, and for fun and curiosity.

Fig 92 Saddle grafting. Left: seed-raised rhododendron rootstock before cutting. Centre bottom: making a wedge cut. Centre top: prepared graft with inverted 'V' cut ready to 'sit' on the wedge. Right: bind with grafting tape. Hold the leaves together with rubber band until new growth appears.

Fig 93 Side grafting. Left: Make a sloping cut half-way through the stem of a seed-raised rootstock. Centre: prepare wedge tipped graft and insert in cut, binding immediately with grafting tape. Right: when new growth appears, cut off the top of the rootstock just above the graft union.

Buy fresh, viable, correctly named seed from a reliable source. Reputable seed houses or firms specializing in the supply of conifer plants and seeds are usually the best bet. Bear in mind that old seed may fail to germinate, as may good seed that has been stored in warm, humid conditions. Where seed cannot be sown immediately, store it in a cool place, no warmer than 40°F(4°C). Keep it dry and out of strong light. Seed of certain varieties may take up to two years to germinate even when good seed is sown under ideal conditions.

The seeds of most conifers need to be subjected to a period of low temperature chilling before they will germinate, and therefore the conventional practice of seed sowing in autumn has much to commend it. Bottom out clean containers with fine chippings, or such as small pieces of polystyrene, for drainage. Ensure that whatever material is used, it is clean and disease-free, and top up with fresh seed compost. Preferably use a soil-based mixture because of the possible time-lag between sowing and germination. John Innes seed compost is excellent for the purpose. Peat-based mixtures can be tricky to handle under these circumstances as they tend to lose condition and turn sour after about six months. Lightly firm the compost so as to leave a minimum ½in(1cm) space at the top. Dust over the compost with grit sand before surface sowing the seeds. Firm them down gently into the grit sand but do not bury. After sowing, water the containers by standing up to half their depth in a dish of clean water until the surface is visibly moist, which usually takes about twenty minutes. As an added precaution against damping off, and other seedling diseases, add a few crystals of potassium permanganate — just sufficient to colour the water pink. After watering, cover the tops of containers with a sheet of clean glass or plastic.

When dealing with autumn and winter sowings, stand containers outdoors in a safe, sheltered, vermin-free spot so that the seeds can be chilled for six to eight weeks. A garden frame or propagating box are near to ideal.

Where sowings are made in spring and natural chilling is unlikely, it is usual to pre-chill seeds before sowing. Soak the seeds in clean water for ten to twelve hours. Strain, and then mix the seeds with a small quantity of damp peat. Put the peat/seed mix into a clean plastic bag and chill for three to eight weeks in a domestic refrigerator before sowing.

Once chilled, move the seeds into warmth to germinate. A temperature of around 60°F(16°C) is needed, rising to no more than 70°F(21°C) maximum. Shade from strong sun and keep the compost moist, but not overwet, at all times. Depending on variety, germination can begin within six weeks or less, but can take up to two years. Where seeds do not germinate during the first season, stand them outdoors again to receive a second chilling for about eight weeks. Then germinate in warmth as before.

Once the seedlings have germinated, give them increased ventilation and pot up into small pots of soil-based potting compost. Protect young plants from frost, hard weather and excessive wet from September to April. At other times of the year stand acclimatized young plants outdoors in a sheltered spot protected from strong midday sun and drying winds. One good way is to stand them inside a netting tunnel of fine mesh netting supported on a light frame and closed at the ends and sides. A netting tunnel provides shade and shelter while ensuring good ventilation. A garden frame with a net cover will achieve the same ends.

Keep young plants well watered and give them an occasional liquid feed. Feeding about once a month while plants are in active growth is sufficient between April and August. Pot on young plants as necessary in spring when roots are seen to encircle the outside of the rootball.

As soon as plants are established and growing freely, and have made sufficient size, they are ready to plant out. It may take anything from two to five years from starting off to planting out, and during this growing on period, syringe over the young plants in the evenings during warm, dry weather. This encourages new growth and helps to keep red spider mites at bay.

CHAPTER 7

Plant Guide

NAMES AND NAME CHANGING

Sooner or later, anyone with an interest in, or an involvement with heathers and conifers comes up against a bewildering array of plant names. The newcomer can be excused for questioning the need for what, at first glance, seems to be an almost incomprehensible system of naming. In practice, most garden plants have a least two names – a formal Latin or botanical full title and one or more popular or local names.

By international convention, the Latin name is, or should be, approved and accepted in any part of the world. When buying plants, or when looking around gardens, the enthusiast should always look for the Latin names. They are sound and reliable. Popular names, which vary from one country to another, or even one district to another, can be very confusing.

Correct naming and labelling are vital for a plant's accurate identification. In turn accurate identification provides important clues as to a plant's ultimate size, shape, needs and distinguishing features – and therefore to its suitability for any given situation.

The heather and conifer enthusiast needs to be alerted to, but not worried by, the fact that occasionally a plant may be known by more than one Latin name. Garden centres, gardeners, and nurseries may use a well-known Latin name for a certain plant whereas botanists may use another. The Mediterranean heath, for example, is known to gardeners and listed in many catalogues as *Erica mediterranea* but is *E. erigena* to botanists and other authorities.

Name changing is an ongoing process. As knowledge advances, re-classification of plants takes place. However, there is an inevitable time lag before new names are generally adopted in gardening circles.

INDIVIDUAL PLANT ENTRIES

The names used in this book are those currently in general use in garden centres and in plant lists in catalogues. They are not necessarily the latest botanically correct names. The first entry is the Latin or botanical name together with variety where appropriate. The popular name follows underneath.

Each plant is given a hardiness rating according to its ability to survive outdoors in a particular area under normal conditions. Plants rated H1 are generally hardy tolerating minimum winter temperatures of 0–10°F (minus 18 to minus 12°C). Plants with an H2 rating are best confined to southern and south western districts and mild sheltered inland gardens. These plants normally survive minimum winter temperatures of 10–20°F (minus 12 to minus 6°C). Plants with an H3 rating are only marginally hardy. They need the protection of a warm wall or other sheltered spot in a southern or south western garden where winter minimum temperatures will not drop below 20–30°F (minus 6 to minus 1°C).

Container-grown plants are less hardy than similar varieties direct planted in beds and borders. Thus plants rated H1 become H2 when grown in containers. Plants normally rated H2 become H3 in containers. And plants rated H3 need indoor protection when overwintered in containers.

HEATHERS AND ALLIES

Andromeda polifolia 'Compacta' (Andromeda, Bog or Marsh Rosemary)

- Evergreen shrublet
- Hardiness – HI
- Care – Average

Description Height 6in(15cm). Spread 12in(30cm). Usually forms a pleasing compact shrublet with upright thin wiry stems and creeping or spreading habit. Clusters of small, dainty pink flowers appear at the tips of each stem starting in May and continuing on throughout summer. The leaves are dark green, leathery and needle-like.
Maturity Flowering usually begins within 1–2 years of planting.

Fig 94   Andromeda polifolia (bog rosemary). This dainty plant is best plunge planted, complete with pot, to avoid being smothered out by more vigorous neighbours.

Lifespan About 5–7 years given reasonable care.
Other varieties *A.p.* 'Major' is a slightly larger form of the above reaching about 16in(40cm) in height with a spread of up to 2ft(60cm).
Uses A first-class ground cover plant for peat bed, raised bed, pocket in rock garden or containers.
Planting Autumn or spring. Set out pot-grown plants preferably in groups of 2, 3 or more allowing about 10in(25cm) between plants. Plant singly in pans or containers.
Position Prefers an open, sunny or partially shaded spot. At its best in a cool, moist climate.
Soil Needs an acid, humus-rich, moist but free-draining root run. Suitable for a bog garden provided the ground is not stagnantly wet. Use lime-free ericaceous potting compost for containers. Resents root disturbance so set out well-grown pot-raised stock.
Propagation Take 3in(8cm) semi-ripe heel or node cuttings during summer. The alternative is to layer in autumn, which takes about 12 months.
Treatment Keep newly set out plants moist and weed-free at all times during the first year or two. If possible use rainwater for irrigation. Repot container plants annually in autumn or spring.
Pruning Not as a rule necessary.
Problems Generally trouble free.

Arctostaphylos uva-ursi (Red Bearberry)

- Evergreen shrublet
- Hardiness – HI
- Care – Easy to average.

Description Height 4in(10cm). Spread 2ft (60cm) or more. Forms a creeping or trailing leafy alpine shrublet with slender stems. The flowers are usually white tinged with pink. They are carried in clusters at the tips of stems in spring and early summer. Currant-like red berries follow the flowers in mid to late summer. The small leaves are dark green and leathery showing off the berries to advantage.

Maturity Flowering and berrying usually start within 1–2 years of planting.

Lifespan Expect about 7–10 years of useful life.

Other varieties This is the main cultivated representative of this genus at the present time.

Uses A good ground cover plant for covering lime-free sandy banks and for infilling in rock gardens. Also suitable for planting in containers.

Planting Set out plants in spring or autumn, ideally in groups. Allow about 12in(30cm) spacing for quick ground cover.

Position A sunny or partially shaded site will suit.

Soil A free-draining acid, sandy soil well enriched with peat gives good results. Use lime-free ericaceous potting compost in containers.

Propagation Take 2in(5cm) semi-ripe heel cuttings in summer and root under cover. Peg down layers in spring and they should be ready for lifting within 12–24 months.

Treatment Keep plants weed-free, moist and well mulched during spring and summer for the first two years at least.

Pruning Not as a rule needed but plants can be clipped around the edges to confine them to their allotted space.

Problems Usually trouble free.

Calluna vulgaris 'Sir John Charrington' (Heather, Ling, Scotch Heather)

- Evergreen shrub
- Hardiness – H1
- Care – Easy to average.

Description Height up to 18in(45cm) but can reach 3ft(90cm). Spread of up to 2ft(60cm) or more. Makes a fairly dense, sometimes straggly, bushy shrub, usually much branched. The long flower spikes are crimson and carried from August to November. The leaves are small, numerous and scale-like. The summer foliage is golden orange. Orange-red tints develop in winter. The fruits are inconspicuous dry seeds.

Maturity Flowering normally begins within 12

Fig 95 Calluna 'Kinlochruel' is a particularly free-flowering variety – provided it is not planted in lime-rich soil.

months of planting. The foliage provides year-round colour from setting out.

Lifespan Expect a useful life of 10 years or more.

Other varieties There are many excellent varieties from which to choose. C.v. 'Golden Carpet' (height 6in(15cm), golden summer foliage turning orange-red in winter and mauve flowers). C.v. 'H. E. Beale' (height 2ft(60cm), double pink flowers and green foliage). C.v. 'Kinlochruel' (height 10in(25cm), double white flowers and green foliage), C.v. 'Silver Knight' (height 12in(30cm), pink flowers and silver-grey foliage), C.v. 'Wickwar Flame' (height 12in(30cm), lavender flowers, orange-red summer foliage and flame-red in winter). All the above varieties flower between August and early November.

Uses First class as ground cover, as edgings to beds and borders, with conifers in mixed beds and borders. Popular as a cut flower – particularly the white varieties.

Planting Set out in spring or autumn. Allow 12in(30cm) between dwarf or compact varieties under 12in(30cm) in height. Increase spacing to 18in(45cm) for taller kinds.

Position Callunas prefer open sunny positions. They tend to become straggly and shy flowering in shade.

Soil Need acid, peaty moist soil that is free-draining and preferably not over-rich. Use lime-free ericaceous potting compost in containers.

Propagation Where only small numbers of plants are required, peg down layers in spring or summer and they should be ready for lifting about 12 months later. Alternatively, take tip cuttings 1–1½in(1–2cm) long during summer and root under cover.

Treatment It is essential to keep young plants well watered and weed-free especially in the first year or two after planting. Mulch young plants each spring.

Pruning Light pruning is the norm. Clip back flowering shoots by a quarter to a third in early winter or spring.

Problems Occasional attacks of heather wilt. In towns, cats can be a nuisance as they foul the plants.

Daboecia cantabrica 'Atropur-purea' (St Dabeoc's Heath, Irish Bell Heather)

- Evergreen shrub
- Hardiness – H2–3
- Care – Easy to average

Description Height and spread 2ft(60cm)–3ft(90cm). Unless kept dense by judicious clipping, tends to form a straggly, open shrub. The bell-shaped, small purple flowers are produced freely, in succession, from late May to October or early November. The small dark-green leaves turn a pleasing bronze-green in winter.

Maturity Flowering normally starts in the first season after planting.

Fig 96 Daboecia cantabrica 'Bi-color'. This unusual acid-loving heath carries white and purple flowers on one plant.

Lifespan A useful lifespan of about 5–7 years is average but it can be considerably more.

Other varieties D. c. 'Alba' is an attractive white flowered form of the above, its winter foliage is more green than bronze. D. c. 'William Buchanan' with a height and spread of 12in(30cm) is smaller and more compact, and has crimson flowers but is otherwise similar to 'Atropurpurea'.

Uses It is valuable in beds and borders, as ground cover, in raised beds, in rock gardens and in containers.

Planting Best set out in spring but autumn is satisfactory. For quick cover plant 15in(38cm) apart in groups.

Position Full sun and an open site is preferred but will adapt to partial light shade.

Soil Thrives in light, acid peaty sandy free-draining but moist soils. use lime-free potting composts for containers and raised beds.

Propagation Take 2in(5cm) semi-ripe cuttings during summer. Peg down layers in spring and they should be ready for lifting within about 12 months.

Treatment Keep young plants weed-free and moist at all times preferably using rainwater for irrigation. Mulch plants annually in spring.

Pruning Clip over plants each spring cutting out any dead or frosted growth back to sound tissue at the same time.

Problems Normally trouble-free apart from occasional damage to new growth by late spring frosts.

Erica arborea 'Alpina' (Tree Heath, Tree Heather)

- Evergreen shrub
- Hardiness – H2–3
- Care – Average

Description Height 10ft(3m). Spread 5–7ft (1.5–2m). Forms a fairly dense bushy, sometimes spikey shrub. Often a stout stem or thick branches will develop with age. Long spikes of fragrant small white flowers are freely produced on mature plants during March and April. The vivid, bright, fresh-green leaves are small and needle-like and provide an excellent foil for the flowers.

Maturity After planting, the shrubs often take 2–3 years to settle down and flower freely.

Lifespan Given suitable growing conditions a useful life of 25 years or more is possible.

Other varieties *E.a.* 'Albert's Gold' – height to 6ft(1.8m) or more. Slower growing and smaller than 'Alpina'. Its main feature is bright gold winter foliage which turns golden-green in summer.

Uses Excellent for hedging and screening and as a nurse crop for more tender plants. Good as a dot or accent plant in beds and borders.

Planting Spring is best, with autumn as an alternative. When planting in rows allow a minimum 3–4ft(1–1.2m) between plants. Give individual specimens more room and allow up to a 5ft(1.5m) spread.

Position An open sunny site sheltered from strong or chilling winds is best. Avoid east-facing sites and damaging early morning sun.

Soil A deep acid, peaty soil, with a good proportion of sand is ideal but this shrub will adapt to alkaline conditions.

Propagation Take semi-ripe 1½in(4cm) cuttings during summer and root under cover.

Treatment Keep young plants weed free, well-watered and mulched in spring and summer. Protect newly set out plants from wind – particularly important during their first winter.

Pruning Shorten back new growths by one-third to a half as soon as flowering is over for the season. This treatment is necessary for the first 3 seasons at least to encourage bushy growth. In subsequent years lightly clip over after flowering to keep shrubs trim and tidy.

Problems Generally healthy, these shrubs occasionally suffer from heather dieback disease.

Erica carnea 'Myretoun Ruby' (Winter Heath)

- Evergreen Shrub
- Hardiness – H1–2
- Care – Easy to average

Description Height 10in(25cm). Spread 18in (45cm). Makes a compact, dense, tufty shrub or shrublet. It becomes increasingly prostrate with age. Glowing ruby-red flowers are produced in succession from late autumn to spring. The dark-green leaves complement the flowers well.

Maturity Flowering begins at an early age. Plants are often set out in full bloom.

Lifespan Average 10–12 years. Longer is possible, given good cultivations.

Other varieties 'Anne Sparkes' – height 10in(25cm), purple-red flowers, orange-yellow foliage tipped bronze red. 'Aurea' – height 10in(25cm), deep pink flowers, golden foliage. 'Foxhollow' – height 6in(15cm), flowers lavender and sparce, summer foliage bright gold-pink and red tinged in winter. 'Springwood White' – height 8in(20cm), flowers white, foliage bright green, vigorous. 'Vivellii' – height 10in(25cm), flowers carmine-pink, foliage bronze, a slow grower, long lived.

Uses *E. carnea* varieties provide excellent ground cover. They are good in rock gardens, raised beds and containers and are excellent in mixed beds and borders interplanted with conifers. They make first-class edgings.

Planting Although planting and final potting is best carried out in autumn or spring, container-grown plants can be set out during mild spells in early winter. Allow about 15in(38cm) between plants.

Position An open, sunny situation is ideal but will adapt to light shade, provided the plants are not under the drips of trees. If possible avoid east-facing sites exposed to early morning sun.

Soil Acid peaty or leafy free-draining soil is best. However, winter heaths will tolerate mildly alkaline conditions. Avoid over-rich soils.

Propagation A popular means of increase is to peg down layers in spring or early autumn. Plants should be ready for lifting about 12 months later. Alternatively take 1–1½in(3–4cm) semi-ripe or green cuttings in summer and root under cover.

Treatment Keep weed-free and well watered, especially during the first year. Mulch annually each spring for the first few years.

Pruning Lightly clip over as the last of the flowers fade. This ensures even, bushy, compact growth. Cut out any dead or diseased shoots whenever seen.

Problems Plants occasionally suffer from heather dieback disease, and from fouling by cats.

Erica cinerea 'White Dale' (Scotch Bell Heather)

- Evergreen Shrub
- Hardiness – H1
- Care – Easy to average

Description Height 12in(30cm). Spread 24in(60cm). A compact, bushy shrub, with stiff much-branched shoots and spreading habit. Masses of pure white, bell-shaped flowers are produced between July and October. The dead, dry flowers are a bonus during winter. The fresh,

Fig 97 Erica cinerea 'Pink Foam' is but one of many varieties of bell heather which dislikes lime. However, it adapts to drier conditions than many heathers.

bright green foliage is made up of small, needle-like leaves.

Maturity Flowering starts early, often before planting out and certainly within 6–9 months of planting or final potting.

Lifespan Tends to be shorter than many others – from 5–8 years. This is more than compensated for by their beauty and free-flowering habit.

Other varieties 'C.D. Eason' height 12in(30cm), red-pink flowers, deep-green foliage. 'Golden Hue' height 10in(25cm), amethyst flowers, foliage gold in summer and red in winter. 'Pink Ice' height 10in(25cm), flowers glowing pink, foliage grey and green with compact habit. 'Purple Beauty' height 10in(25cm), flowers bright purple, foliage dark green. Vigorous. 'Velvet Night' height 12in(30cm), flowers purple-black, foliage mid-green. All the above varieties have a spread of up to 24in (60cm).

Uses First class in beds, borders, rock gardens, raised beds and containers, either singly or massed.

Planting Plant out and pot up in autumn or

spring. Set out plants about 18in(45cm) apart in groups. Single plants in pockets will comfortably fill a 20in(50cm) spread in all directions.

Position An open, sunny situation is best. Adapts to warm, dryish climates better than most heathers.

Soil Thrives in acid soils and suffers in those of an alkaline nature. A free-draining light peaty root run is ideal. Adapts to drier soils than is the norm for heathers. Use lime-free potting composts in containers.

Propagation Peg down layers in spring to produce rooted layers within 12 months. Alternatively take 1½in(4cm) cuttings of current season's growth in summer and root under cover.

Treatment Keep weed-free and well watered during the first year or two especially in dry conditions. Mulch annually.

Pruning Clip over plants each spring to neaten off and remove old flower heads. Cut out any dead or damaged shoots on sight.

Problems Occasional attacks by heather dieback disease. Possible fouling by cats.

Erica x darleyensis 'Darley Dale'
(Winter Heath)

- Evergreen Shrub
- Hardiness – HI–2
- Care – Easy to average

Description Height 2ft(60cm). Spread 2½ft(75cm). Makes a dense, bushy, rounded shrub of neat, pleasing habit. The long spikes of flowers are soft mauve-pink and very freely produced. A very long flowering season – blooming normally begins in late October and continues through to early May. The small needle-shaped leaves are mid-dark green.

Maturity Flowering normally begins within 12 months of planting, gradually increasing in profusion each year until fully mature in 3–4 years.

Lifespan Give reasonable care and expect a useful life of 20–25 years.

Other varieties 'A. T. Johnson' height 2–3ft(60–90cm), flowers magenta and prolific

Fig 98 Erica x darleyensis – *a bold spring and early summer flowering plant – grows well on most average soils.*

and reliable, foliage light bright green and conspicuous; vigorous. 'Ghost Hills' height 2ft(60cm), flowers deep rose; foliage mid-green with cream-tipped new shoots. 'Jack H. Brummage' height 2ft(60cm), flowers pink, foliage golden. 'Silver Beads' a white flowered form of 'Darley Dale'.

Uses Outstanding as ground cover in beds and borders and for cutting. Good as a specimen and for use as a dot or accent plant. Young plants are suitable for plunge planting in containers.

Planting Set out in autumn or spring. Space plants about 20in(50cm) apart in groups. Single specimens need about 2ft(60cm) spread in all directions.

Position A sunny open situation is best. Avoid exposure to freezing cold north or east winds.

Soil Grows well in almost any average soil with a high organic content provided it is not too rich in nutrients. Adapts to free-draining clay soils. Unlike most other heathers seems to grow and flower well on alkaline soils.

Propagation Take semi-ripe 1½in(4cm) cuttings in summer and root under cover.

Treatment Keep young plants weed-free, well-watered and mulched throughout spring and summer. Protect newly planted stock from wind.

Pruning Clip over annually in May as soon as flowering is over.

Problems Can suffer from heather dieback.

Erica mediterranea 'Brightness' (syns E. erigena and E. hibernica) (Mediterranean Heath)

- Evergreen Shrub
- Hardiness – H2
- Care – Easy to average

Description Height 3ft(90cm). Spread 3ft (90cm). Makes a medium sized, dense, bushy, much branched shrub. It is grown primarily for the beauty of its flowers. The succession of purplish-red buds are followed by sweet scented rose-pink bell-shaped flowers to provide colour from late February through to May. The foliage is typically heather-like and is dark-green with needle-shaped leaves.

Fig 99 Erica mediterranea 'W. T. Rackliff' – makes a fairly big spring flowering plant which does well on most soils of average fertility.

Maturity Usually commences flowering in the first flowering season after planting but it takes about 3 years or so to get well established and flower freely.

Lifespan Reasonably expect 15 years or more of useful life given good cultivations.

Other varieties 'Golden Lady' height to 18in(45cm), white May–June flowers, golden evergreen foliage. 'Irish Dusk' height to 2ft(60cm), pink flowered from November to May, grey foliage. 'Superba' height to 7ft(2m), deep-pink scented flowers from March to May, foliage dark-green. 'W. T. Rackliff' height to 2ft(60cm), white flowers from January to April, dense neat dark-green foliage.

Uses Tall varieties make good specimen and accent plants and are useful for hedging. Other varieties are excellent as ground cover in beds and borders, in raised beds and in the rock garden.

Planting Plant out in spring or autumn. Allow 18in(45cm) between plants for compact varieties. Give hedging a 2ft(60cm) spacing.

Position Needs an open sunny site with some shelter from cold or drying winds.

Soil Grows well in most average soils provided they are free-draining, well enriched with peat and not too rich in nutrients. Adapts to alkaline as well as acid and neutral soils.

Propagation Peg down layers in spring or take 1½in(4cm) semi-ripe cuttings during summer and root under cover.

Treatment Keep weed-free, well watered and mulched during the first year or two at least. Protect newly set out plants from drying winds at least during the first winter and spring after planting.

Pruning Clip over annually each spring to remove dead flower heads and keep plants tidy. Shorten back new growth on hedging plants by a third to a half in late spring for the first 3 years. Subsequently resort to a light spring clipping. Fail to cut back initially and you risk bare stems at the base.

Problems Generally trouble free apart from an occasional attack of heather wilt.

Erica tetralix 'Con Underwood'
(Cross-leaved Heath)

- Evergreen Shrub
- Hardiness – H2
- Care – Easy

Description Height 10in(25cm). Spread 18in(45cm). Makes a neat, bushy, hummocky mound. The crimson bell-shaped flowers are produced over a long period from June to October. They are carried in terminal clusters at the tips of shoots. The foliage is a pleasing grey-green.

Maturity Flowering begins early often before plants are set out in their final positions.

Lifespan A minimum useful life of 7–10 years is about the norm given average garden conditions.

Other varieties *E.t.* 'Alba Mollis' height 12in(30cm), similar to above, makes a slightly larger plant with white flowers. *E.t.* 'Hookstone Pink' height 12in(30cm), an excellent pink flowered variety with silver-grey foliage.

Uses Excellent as ground cover in beds and borders planted en-masse. A valuable edging plant. Useful in the rock garden planted singly or in groups.

Planting Preferably set out plants in spring especially if the soil is cold or wet. Allow about 15in(38cm) between plants set out in groups. Allow 12in(30cm) when used as edging.

Position Grows best in open sunny sites sheltered from cold or drying winds from the east. Does particularly well in western and south-western districts.

Soil Moist, acid, free-draining soil is preferred. Suffers in dry soils and is intolerant of alkaline soil.

Propagation Peg down vigorous 1–2 year old layers in spring. Expect rooting within 12 months. Take 1–1½in(3–4cm) semi-ripe cuttings during summer and root under cover.

Treatment Keep weed-free and well watered. These heathers must never be allowed to dry out. Mulch annually each spring, at least until well established.

Pruning Clip over in spring each year, rather than immediately after flowering, thus maximizing on winter effects.

Problems Dryness is a potential hazard but otherwise relatively trouble free.

Erica vagans 'Mrs D. F. Maxwell'
(Cornish Heath)

- Evergreen Shrub
- Hardiness – H2
- Care – Easy to average

Description Height 20in(50cm) but can reach 3ft(90cm). Spread 2ft(60cm) but can reach 3½ft (1m). Forms a rounded or spreading shrub, which tends to sprawl if not kept in shape by regular pruning. Bell-shaped, rose-cerise flowers are produced in succession from July to October/early November. As they fade they brown and then persist as a bonus through winter. The narrow needle-shaped leaves are a pleasing bright green.

Maturity Free-flowering starts within 12 months of planting.

Lifespan Given care – at least 15 years.

Other varieties *E.v.* 'Lyonesse' height 20in(50cm), outstanding with white flowers, yellow anthers and bright green foliage. *E.v.* 'St Keverne' height 20in(50cm), clear pink flowers and dark-green foliage. *E.v.* 'Valery Proudley' height 10in(25cm), white flowers and golden foliage.

Uses Versatile and suitable for specimen and accent plants massing as ground cover in beds and borders, low hedging, raised beds, rock gardens, and containers.

Planting Plant in spring or autumn or during mild spells in winter provided container-grown stock are used. For ground cover set plants 18in(45cm) apart. Set dwarf varieties and hedging closer at 15in(38cm).

Position An open sunny site not too exposed to cold or drying winds is preferred. Flourishes in coastal districts.

Soil Thrives in moist, well-drained, acid peaty soil that is not over-rich in nutrients. Adapts well to slightly alkaline conditions if the soil is not too

Fig 100 Erica vagans 'Mrs Maxwell' – give this summer flowering variety acid soil. It likes moisture and flourishes by the waterside as here.

shallow. Use lime-free potting compost in containers.

Propagation   Peg down layers in spring or early autumn and plants should be ready for lifting within 12 months. Take 1–1½in(3–4cm) semi-ripe or green cuttings in summer and root under cover.

Treatment   Protect specimen plants from wind during their first winter. Keep weed-free and well watered. Do not allow these moisture-loving heathers to dry out. Mulch annually each spring.

Pruning   Clip over in spring rather than immediately after flowering so as to maximize winter effects.

Problems   Dryness is a potential threat.

Pernettya mucronata 'Bell's Seedling' (Pernettya)

- Evergreen Shrub
- Hardiness – H1–2
- Care – Easy to average

Description   Height 3ft(90cm) or 4ft(1.2m) plus in shade. Spread 4ft(1.2m). Normally a fairly dense, thicket-forming shrub with red wiry stems. Plant clumps will continue to enlarge and spread indefinitely. White heather-like flowers are freely produced during May and June. These are followed by bright red berries which colour up in August and persist through to March or early April. Shiny dark-green leaves show off both flowers and berries to good effect.

Maturity   Flowering and berrying may not make any appreciable impact for at least 2–3 years after planting but thereafter the shrub will improve yearly.

Lifespan   Expect a useful life of 25 years plus given suitable growing conditions.

Other varieties   Similar in size, habit and flower to the above are *P.m.* 'Pink Pearl', lilac-pink berries and *P.m.* 'White Pearl' gleaming white berries. *P. prostrata pentlandii* a closely related creeping species; height and spread to 12in(30cm) with white flowers and black berries.

99

Fig 101   Pernettya mucronata 'Pink Pearl'. A gardenworthy, acid-loving ground cover plant with a long season of interest.

Uses   Effective as ground cover in beds and borders and for underplanting in light shade.

Planting   Plant in spring or autumn. Allow 2ft(60cm) between plants. With *P. mucronata* varieties set out in groups of three or more and include 1 male to 3 or 4 female plants. This ensures a full set of berries.

Position   Sun preferred but adapts to light partial shade. Needs shelter from freezing east and north winds.

Soil   Needs acid, free-draining soil of average fertility. Cool, moist peaty root runs are best.

Propagation   Take semi-ripe cuttings in summer and root under cover. Alternatively divide clumps in autumn or spring. Always ensure male and female plants.

Treatment   Keep weed-free, well watered and mulched when young.

Pruning   Little is needed. Shorten straggly shoots in spring. Shorten back tall stems on old plants by a third to encourage new growth.

Problems   Likely to suffer from chlorosis on alkaline soils but otherwise trouble free.

Pieris japonica 'Variegata'
(Andromeda Pieris)

- Evergreen Shrub
- Hardiness – H2–3
- Care – Easy to average

Description   Height   3ft(90cm).   Spread 3ft(90cm). An outstandingly attractive rounded, bushy slow-growing shrub. The pitcher-shaped white flowers resemble lily of the valley and are carried in terminal racemes in March and April. The glossy, variegated creamy white, flushed pink leaves provide year-round colour.

Maturity   Expect flowering within a year or two of planting, the foliage is of interest immediately.

Lifespan   30 plus years of useful life is the norm.

Other varieties *P.* 'Forest Flame' height 7ft(2m), an eyecatching bushy shrub with bright red new leaves and white flowers.

Uses   In mild districts makes a good specimen plant and a first-class accent plant in beds and borders. Also looks well on a west-facing wall, suitably shaded from hot sun.

Planting   Plant out in spring or autumn. Allow each plant a minimum 3ft(90cm) spread in all directions. Allow 5ft(1.5m) for *P.* 'Forest Flame'.

Position   Needs a lightly shaded, sheltered site.

Soil   Grows well in almost any acid soil but prefers moist, peaty yet free-draining soil.

Propagation   Take semi-ripe cuttings in summer and root under cover.

Treatment   In the first winter provide a mulch to give roots extra frost protection. Also protect from drying winds and frost with such as netting. Spray over leaves in the evening during hot, dry weather and use rainwater. Keep weed-free, well watered and mulched during the growing season.

Pruning Little needed apart from keeping bushes tidy and dead-heading young plants.
Problems Normally trouble free.

Rhododendron kieskei
(Rhododendron)

- Evergreen or semi-evergreen shrub
- Hardiness – H3
- Care – Easy to average

Description Height 2ft(60cm). Spread 3ft(90cm). Dwarf, bushy, semi-prostrate shrub noted for its unusual yellow flowers which bloom from March to May. The leaves are dark green and fully evergreen in mild climate areas.
Maturity Often flowers within 12 months of planting.
Lifespan An effective useful life in the region of 20 years plus.
Other varieties No readily obtainable varieties of the above. *R. impeditum* height 12in(30cm), spread 20in(50cm) makes a neat dome-shaped shrublet with evergreen foliage and has blue flowers in April and May. The grey-green leaves are aromatic.
Uses Excellent in rock gardens and raised beds.
Planting Plant in spring, with autumn as an alternative. Allow each plant a minimum 3ft(90cm) square.
Position A sheltered, partially shaded spot not exposed to midday sun is recommended. A west-facing aspect is ideal.
Soil A moist, acid, peaty soil gives best results. Dislikes alkaline conditions.
Propagation Peg down layers in spring or autumn for lifting 18 months to 2 years later. Alternatively graft into seedling rootstocks, under cover, during spring.
Treatment Protect young plants against wind and frost during the first winter after planting. Keep weed-free, well watered and mulched.
Pruning None required beyond dead heading (take care not to remove the following year's flower buds) and shortening back straggly or frosted shoots in spring.

Problems Occasionally attacked by weevils and caterpillars. May suffer from chlorosis on alkaline soils.

Vaccinium vitis-idaea (Cowberry)

- Evergreen shrublet
- Hardiness – H1–2
- Care – Easy to average

Description Height 6in(15cm). Spread 18in (45cm). A prostrate, creeping, ground-hugging, mound-forming shrublet. Bell-shaped, small pink-tinged white or pink flowers are produced in succession in terminal racemes between June and August. Small red currant-like edible

Fig 102 Vaccinium vitis idaea (cowberry) – a low growing, acid-loving plant which does well in sun or shade.

berries follow in autumn and early winter. The leaves are small, leathery, dark green and glossy.

Maturity Plants are normally almost on the point of flowering when they are set out.

Lifespan Expect a useful garden life of 10 years.

Other varieties V. vitis-idaea 'Koralle' height 8in(20cm) is an excellent variety of similar habit to the above. Rich pink flowers are followed by coral-red edible berries.

Uses First class as low growing ground cover and as underplanting in light shade. Useful in peat pockets and raised beds.

Planting Plant out in spring or autumn. Allow 15in(38cm) between plants each way. Single plants need an area of about 18in(45cm) square.

Position An open or partly shaded situation.

Soil Needs acid conditions. A free-draining, peaty, moist and not too rich soil is preferred.

Propagation Take root divisions in spring.

Treatment Keep weed-free, well watered and mulched in the first year after planting. Use rain water or lime-free soft water for irrigation.

Pruning Little needed beyond trimming around the edges of plants or plant groups to keep them within their allotted area.

Problems Likely to suffer from chlorosis in alkaline conditions. Otherwise fairly trouble free.

LARGE AND QUICK-GROWING CONIFERS

For 'Treatment' it is assumed that all shrubs are kept weed-free, well watered and mulched during the first few years after planting. Reference is only made to this aspect of care when absolutely vital to success.

Abies koreana (Korean Fir)

- Evergreen tree
- Hardiness – H2
- Care – Easy

Description Height 7ft(2m) in 10 years, ultimately 30ft(9m) plus. Spread 4ft(1.2m) in 10

years, ultimately to 20ft(6m) plus. A bushy, conical tree of neat outline and fairly densely textured foliage. The needle-shaped leaves are dark green with white undersides. The cylindrical purple fir-cones are noteworthy. They are to be found during autumn, even on small trees of 3ft(90cm) or less. The profusion of red or pink female spring flowers carried on mature trees are quite something.

Maturity Despite the slow to moderate growth rate, flowering and cone production begins within 3–5 years of planting.

Lifespan Expect a garden life of 40 years plus given good growing conditions.

Other varieties A.k. 'Aurea' is a choice golden-leaved form. It is slower growing than the above.

Uses A useful specimen tree for lawn areas.

Planting Plant out in autumn or spring. Spring is preferred in cold or wet winter areas. Allow a minimum 5ft(1.5m) spread. Do not plant closer to buildings than 20ft(6m) – this is vital on heavy soils. Aim to plant small trees of about 12in(30cm) in height as they re-establish better and more quickly than larger stock.

Position Grows well in sun or partial light shade but the golden-leaved variety needs sun. Shelter from freezing east or north winds.

Soil An acid to neutral, free-draining yet moist light soil preferred. Adapts to mildly alkaline conditions if the soil is not too shallow.

Propagation Sow the seed of A. koreana in autumn or winter. Pre-chill for 8 weeks before germinating in warmth under cover. Graft the golden-leaved variety under cover in spring onto seedling rootstocks.

Pruning Little needed. Shorten straggly shoots. Where forking occurs, remove secondary leaders to limit the tree to one central stem.

Problems Occasionally attacked by adelges.

Araucaria araucana (Monkey Puzzle)

- Evergreen tree
- Hardiness – H1–2
- Care – Easy

Description Height 20ft(6m) in 20 years. Spread 10ft(3m) in 20 years. Height and spread can ultimately double or treble in favourable situations. A spectacular, large open conical or rounded spreading tree. The trunk is stiffly erect. Very slow growing when young, putting on about 4in(10cm) a year, increasing to about 12in(30cm) per annum when 10 years old. Trees become round topped or domed with age and with downswept lower branches. The leaves are glossy, dark green and arranged spirally on the branches. Large cones are produced on mature, female trees in favourable surroundings.

Maturity A distinctive foliage tree from the day of planting. Cones are rarely produced until middle age.

Lifespan 60 years plus is the norm in favourable situations.

Other varieties None.

Uses Essentially a specimen tree for grass areas.

Planting Spring planting is best. Avoid planting nearer to buildings than 30ft(9m) and allow at least a 30ft(9m) square of clear space.

Position Suits sun, adapts to semi-shade and prefers not to be too exposed. A mild, moist climate is best.

Soil Prefers a deep, free-draining soil of average fertility.

Propagation Plants can be raised from 4in(10cm) tip cuttings, taken in summer and rooted in warmth. Alternatively, sow seeds indoors in spring.

Pruning Little or none required beyond cutting back any dead or damaged growths.

Problems Normally trouble free.

Cedrus atlantica glauca (Blue Cedar)

- Evergreen tree
- Hardiness – H2
- Care – Easy to average

Description Height 12ft(3.5m) in 10 years, ultimately up to 60ft(18m) plus. Spread 5ft(1.5m)

Fig 103 *Blue cedar (Cedrus atlantica glauca) – the attractive cones are often overlooked on large mature trees.*

in 10 years, ultimately to 25ft(7.5m) plus. Open, sparsely branched and pyramidal when, young. As trees age they become increasingly flat topped with outstretched, slightly ascending branches. The needle-shaped leaves are an intense silvery blue making a most striking tree. Blue-green cones ripen to brown and are produced at maturity.

Maturity The foliage is immediately attractive. Expect cones after about 20 years.

Lifespan In favourable situations lives for upwards of 150 years.

Other varieties *C.a.* 'Glauca Pendula' height to 25ft(7.5m) is a smaller weeping version of the above.

Uses Essentially a specimen tree for the larger garden.

Planting Set out in autumn or spring. Plant trees at least 50ft(15m) away from buildings or other structures.

Position Thrives in a warm, sunny situation which is not too exposed.

Soil Grown satisfactorily in most free-draining soils of average fertility including those containing some lime.

Propagation The best coloured forms, and

weeping kinds, are grafted indoors onto seed-raised rootstocks in spring. Sow seeds under cover for raising rootstocks or for fun.
Treatment Stake and tie newly planted trees.
Pruning Little is needed beyond limiting the tree to one main stem. Cut out any secondary leaders if forking occurs.
Problems Generally trouble free.

Cedrus deodara 'Aurea' (Golden Deodar)

- Evergreen tree
- Hardiness – H2–3
- Care – Average

Description Height 10ft(3m) in 10 years, ultimately to 30ft(9m) plus. Spread 5ft(1.5m), ultimately to 12ft(3.5m). A very graceful, outstandingly attractive, pyramidal, densely foliaged tree with arching or pendent branch tips. With age the top tends to become increasingly flattened with drooping or pendulous leaders. The new season's spring foliage is golden turning to yellowish-green by autumn. Old trees occasionally carry brown cones.
Maturity The foliage provides instant appeal from planting time but it becomes increasingly impressive as the tree gains in size. Cone bearing begins at 40 years plus.
Lifespan A useful life of 50 years is possible given favourable conditions.
Other varieties *C.d.* 'Golden Horizon' is a similar sized though wider and more spreading tree. The golden colouring persists year round.
Uses A first-class specimen tree for the medium to large garden.
Planting Plant in autumn or spring. Do not plant closer to buildings than 25ft(7.5m). Allow this tree sufficient space to be seen to advantage.
Position At its best in a sheltered situation in a mild climate planted in semi-shade.
Soil Grows well in any free-draining soil of average fertility. Adapts to alkaline soils.
Propagation Graft under cover in spring onto seed-raised rootstocks in slight warmth.

Treatment Stake and tie newly planted trees until established.
Pruning Little is needed beyond limiting the tree to a single leader. If forking occurs remove any secondary main stems. Shorten any straggly or misplaced stems. If needed, pruning is best carried out in late spring.
Problems More or less trouble free.

Chamaecyparis lawsoniana 'Ellwoodii' (Lawson Cypress)

- Evergreen shrub or tree
- Hardiness – H1–2
- Care – Easy

Description Height 7ft(2m) in 10 years, ultimately to 15ft(4.5m) plus. Spread 2½ft(75cm) in 10 years, ultimately to 5ft(1.5m) plus. Of compact habit, closely branched from ground level upwards. The shape varies from pyramidal to columnar depending in part on whether the plant is single or multi-stemmed. The dense, feathery grey-green summer foliage turns to a blue-green in winter. Mature plants carry insignificant blue-green or brown small rounded cones.
Maturity The foliage is attractive from the start. The small cones are not produced for at least 10 years after planting.
Lifespan A useful garden life of 70–100 years is not uncommon.
Other varieties *C.l.* 'Lanei Aurea', a golden foliaged conical variety reaching an ultimate height of 30ft(9m). *C.l.* 'Pembury Blue', a silver-blue foliaged conical or pyramidal variety reaching an ultimate height of 40ft(12m).
Uses Suitable as single specimens grouped with other conifers, as accent plants with such as heathers, for screening and as a container plant.
Planting Plant in spring or autumn. Do not plant closer to a building than a distance equal to the ultimate height of the tree.
Position Blue and gold varieties need sun while others will adapt to partial shade. Avoid very exposed spots.
Soil Flourishes in any free-draining, moist soil of

average fertility including those of an alkaline or heavy nature. Use standard soil-based potting compost for containers.

Propagation Take semi-ripe or green cuttings in early autumn and root under cover.

Pruning Minimal pruning apart from shortening back straggly shoots and cutting out surplus leaders where forking occurs. Unless multi-stemmed trees are the aim, leave only one main stem. Remove the tops to restrain the height.

Problems Once established, trouble free.

Chamaecyparis pisifera 'Boulevard'
(Sawara Cypress)

- Evergreen tree
- Hardiness – H2–3
- Care – Easy to average

Description Height 5ft(1.5m) in 10 years, ultimately to 15ft(4.5m). Spread 3ft(90cm) in 10 years, ultimately to 8ft(2.5m). A conical, densely foliaged bushy tree becoming more round topped with age. The foliage is a striking blue-silver, blue-green with a lustrous sheen on the minute, numerous, leaflets. Not usually cone bearing.

Maturity Foliage colour provides interest from the start.

Lifespan If left to attain full size, a useful life of 40 years is possible.

Other varieties C.p. 'Plumosa Aurea', height and spread to 4ft(1.2m) in 10 years; ultimate height to 25ft(7.5m), spread to 12ft(3.5m). Conical becoming columnar with age. The foliage is feathery and fluffy, bright gold when new but bronzing in a matter of weeks.

Uses Excellent as specimens, good as accent plants in beds and borders and useful in mixed conifer/heather groupings. When small, useful for rock gardens and raised beds.

Planting Plant out in autumn in free-draining light soils and favoured sites. Stick to spring planting on heavy soils and less than ideal sites. Do not plant closer to buildings than three-quarters ultimate height – 12ft(3.5m) for 'Boulevard' or 20ft(6m) for 'Plumosa Aurea'.

Position Prefers a semi-shaded, sheltered situation and protection from freezing north or east winds.

Soil Needs a moist, acid to neutral soil that is free-draining and of average fertility.

Propagation Take semi-ripe or green cuttings in early autumn and root under cover.

Treatment Extra temporary shelter from wind needed for the first winter or two.

Pruning Minimal pruning, apart from shortening back straggly shoots and cutting out surplus leaders where forking occurs. Unless multi-stemmed trees are the aim, leave only one main stem. C.p. 'Boulevard' can be kept at about 5ft(1.5m) by removing the growing point of the main leader, and then of subsequent growths.

Problems Once established, trouble free.

Cryptomeria japonica 'Elegans'
(Japanese Cedar)

- Evergreen tree
- Hardiness – H2–3
- Care – Easy to average

Description Height 10ft(3m) in 10 years, ultimately to 15ft(4.5m). Spread 5ft(1.5m) in 10 years, ultimately to 7ft(2m). Of dense, bushy upright habit with very attractive foliage at most times of year. It is dainty, light and feathery, green or light brown in summer, becoming coppery bronze to crimson brown in winter. Inclined to forking. Unless corrected this results in a multi-stemmed tree or bush. Small brown, rounded cones are carried on mature trees late in life.

Maturity Considerable foliage interest from planting stage onwards. Cone bearing begins at about 12 years.

Lifespan A garden life of 35 years plus can be reasonably expected given good conditions.

Other varieties C.j. 'Sekkan Sugi' height to 7ft(2m), spread 3ft(90cm). A much-branched, bushy plant with creamy white new summer growth and ivory, bronze and green winter shadings.

Uses Mainly used as specimens, as accent

plants, for grouping with other conifers or in mixed plantings with heathers and the like. *C.j.* 'Elegans' is also effective for visual screening.

Planting Preferably plant in spring. Do not plant *C.j.* 'Elegans' any nearer to buildings than 15ft(4.5m).

Position Prefers a sunny but well-sheltered spot. A west or south-west-facing aspect is best. Adapts to partial light shade but expect growth to be slower and less compact.

Soil Needs an acid to neutral soil and prefers one which is moist yet free-draining and of average fertility.

Preparation Take semi-ripe or green cuttings in autumn and root under cover.

Treatment Easy to grow if needs are met. Frost, strong or cold winds and dryness are the main hazards. Give temporary protection against wind during first winter in problem gardens. Keep well watered and mulch throughout the early years.

Pruning Little needed. Shorten any damaged or frosted shoots and remove any outworn lower branches. If forking occurs cut out secondary leaders in early summer.

Problems Largely trouble free.

Cupressocyparis leylandii 'Castlewellan' (Leyland Cypress)

- Evergreen tree
- Hardiness – H2
- Easy to demanding

Description Height 25ft(7.5m) in 10 years, ultimately to 60ft(18m). Spread 7ft(2m), ultimately to 15ft(4.5m). A very quick-growing, dense pyramidal or columnar tree noted for its vigour and golden foliage. With regular clipping, forms a close-knit textured plant of almost architectural quality. Cones are not a feature.

Maturity The foliage provides instant effect. Puts on up to 3ft(90cm) in height per annum.

Lifespan Useful garden life is normally in the region of 60 years plus.

Other varieties *x C.l.* 'Robinson's Gold' is

brighter gold than 'Castlewellan' *x C. notabilis* is a grey-green foliaged variety. Both varieties are similar in size and form to the above.

Uses Make bold specimens for the larger garden. Mainly used for formal and semi-formal hedging and screening. Suitable for both coastal and inland gardens.

Planting Spring planting usually results in a more rapid establishment. Do not plant specimens nearer to buildings or drains than 50ft(15m) if unrestricted. Hedges limited to 6ft(1.8m) in height can be planted to within 8ft(2.5m) in safety. Space hedging plants about 3ft(90cm) apart.

Position Sunny, open situations result in good foliage colour. Adapts to partial shade but the foliage is less compact than in sun.

Soil Grows well in most free-draining soils of average fertility. Best in deep, rich, moist soils. Tolerant of moderately alkaline soils.

Propagation Take semi-ripe or green cuttings in early autumn and root under cover.

Treatment Support individual plants of 18in(45cm) and over at planting time until established.

Pruning Restrict specimen trees to a single stem. Allow hedging to reach 12in(30cm) above desired height before cutting out the tops. Clip the sides annually to ensure dense foliage both before and after topping. Carry out all pruning during late spring and summer.

Problems Normally trouble free.

Cupressus macrocarpa 'Goldcrest' (Monterey Cypress)

- Evergreen tree
- Hardiness – H2–3
- Care – Easy to average

Description Height 10ft(3m) at 10 years, ultimately to 40ft(12m) plus. Spread 4ft(1.2m) at 10 years, ultimately to 15ft(4.5m) plus. Of much-branched habit and conical outline when young gradually becoming flat topped and spreading with age. The feathery plume-like sprays of aromatic dense golden foliage are the main attraction. Small rounded brown cones are produced on mature trees.

Maturity The golden foliage is pleasing onwards from planting.

Lifespan In mild districts a life in excess of 50 years is possible.

Other varieties *C.m.* 'Golden Pillar' is similar to above but columnar and narrower.

Uses Especially valuable in mild coastal areas as specimens and as screening.

Planting Plant in spring or autumn. Keep specimen trees and tall screen plants a minimum 30ft(9m) from buildings and allow 8ft(2.5m) for 7ft(2m) high hedging. Space hedging and screening plants no closer than 3ft(1m) apart.

Position Best in full sun and open situations and must have protection from freezing north and east winds.

Soil Grows well in most free-draining soils of average fertility including those of an alkaline nature. Best in deep, rich, moist soils.

Propagation Take semi-ripe or green cuttings in early autumn and root under cover.

Treatment Support individual plants of 18in(45cm) and over at planting time until established.

Pruning Restrict specimen trees to a single stem. Allow hedging to reach 12in(30cm) above desired height before cutting out the tops. Clip the sides annually to ensure dense foliage both before and after topping. Carry out all pruning during late spring and summer.

Problems Normally trouble free.

Ginkgo biloba (Maidenhair Tree)

- Deciduous tree
- Hardiness – H2
- Care – Easy to average

Description Height 12ft(3.5m) in 10 years, ultimately to 30ft(9m). Spread 5ft(1.5m) in 10 years ultimately to 12ft(3.5m). A somewhat narrow, stiff and gaunt – yet not unattractive – young tree, which becomes more spreading with age. The pale green leaves are fan-shaped like

Fig 104 *The curious fan-shaped leaves of* Ginkgo biloba *(maidenhair tree) differ from those of most other conifers. They turn yellow in autumn before falling.*

the leaflets of the maidenhair fern. In autumn they turn butter-yellow before they eventually fall. Although yellow plum-shaped fruits are occasionally seen on female trees, they are not a major attraction.

Maturity The leaves are attractive from planting time onwards. Fruit bearing does not begin for many years on this slow-growing tree.

Lifespan A long-lived tree which lasts for upwards of 100 years.

Other varieties *G.b.* 'Fastigiata' is a narrow erect tree of similar height and features to the above but is altogether more slender.

Uses Mainly used as a specimen but where space allows useful to include in groupings of large conifers.

Planting Plant in autumn or spring. Do not plant nearer to buildings than 30ft(9m), and allow sufficient room for trees to reach their full final spread. Avoid root disturbance as much as possible. To obtain fruit, plant both male and female trees.

Position Grows best in warm, sunny situations protected from damaging cold winds. Adapts to partial shade but growth is slower.

Soil Flourishes in most free-draining soils of average fertility including those of an alkaline or heavy nature.

Propagation Sow fresh seed in autumn or early winter. However, to be sure of male and female plants of *G. biloba* or to ensure *G.b.* 'Fastigiata' comes true to form, grafting in spring onto seedling rootstocks is the norm.

Pruning Pruning, apart from the removal or shortening of dead or damaged wood, is harmful and often results in dying back. Paint over wounds, irrespective of size, with sealing compound.

Problems Normally trouble free.

Juniperus communis 'Hibernica' (syn 'Stricta') (Irish Juniper)

- Evergreen tree or shrub
- Hardiness – H1
- Care – Easy

Description Height 7ft(2m) at 10 years, ultimately to 12ft(3.5m) plus. Spread 2ft(60cm) at 10 years, ultimately to 4ft(1.2m) plus. Develops into an erect, slender pyramidal or columnar tree or shrub, clothed down to ground level with dense prickly foliage. The foliage is slightly aromatic and made up of small, bluish-green leaves with a whitish or pale green reverse. Mature plants carry small blue-black berries.

Maturity Foliage and shape of this slow-growing conifer are interesting from the start. Expect berrying within 5–7 years.

Lifespan Usually long lived, a useful life of 70–100 years is not uncommon.

Other varieties *J.c.* 'Golden Shower', height to 5ft(1.5m) at 10 years, a promising new golden-leaved form of similar shape to the above. *J.c. suecica* (Swedish juniper) is similar in colour, size and shape but has more open foliage and drooping tips to branchlets.

Uses Make good specimens used singly or in pairs to frame views and doorways. Useful for including in group plantings of mixed conifers. Good for screening and look well as accent plants amongst heathers. Useful in containers.

Planting Plant in autumn or spring. Keep plants at least 10ft(3m) away from buildings and allow 20in(50cm) in the case of hedging and screening. Allow specimen and accent plants enough space to grow to maximum spread.

Position Best in a warm, sunny site, especially the golden form but will adapt to light partial shade. Preferably avoid very exposed positions.

Soil Grows well in most free-draining soils of average fertility including those of an alkaline or heavy nature. Use soil-based compost in containers.

Propagation Take semi-ripe or green cuttings in early autumn and root under cover. Plants can be raised from seed sown in autumn under cover but will be variable. Useful for bonsai.

Treatment Although tolerant of dry soils once established, keep newly set out plants well watered during the first year or two.

Pruning Little is needed apart from pruning to shape in late spring or early summer. Where a single stem tree is required, correct any tendency to forking.

Problems Occasionally attacked by juniper scale insects and by caterpillars.

Juniperus x media 'Pfitzerana' (Pfitzer Juniper)

- Evergreen shrub
- Hardiness – H2
- Care – Easy to average

Description Height 3ft(90cm) at 10 years, ultimately to 10ft(3m). Spread 5ft(1.5m) at 10 years, ultimately to 15ft(4.5m). A very distinctive and attractive vase-shaped shrub with ascending, outstretched branches growing outwards and upwards at about 45 degrees. The foliage is a pleasing rich green drooping slightly at the tips. Berries are absent or sparce.

Maturity Pleasing foliage from the outset.

Lifespan Expect a life of at least 40 years.

Other varieties *J. x m.* 'Pfitzerana Aurea' is a most attractive gold-leaved form of the above, slightly less vigorous and a bit smaller.

Uses Popular as a lawn specimen, as a focal point in corners and as camouflage for manhole covers. Reserve for the larger garden.

Planting Preferably plant in spring. Avoid planting closer to buildings than 8ft(2.5m). Allow plants room to grow to full spread but underplanting near branch extremities is possible.

Position Good in sun or partial shade but benefits from shelter.

Soil Thrives in most well-drained but moist soils of average fertility including those of an alkaline and even heavy nature.

Propagation Take semi-ripe or green cuttings in early autumn and root under cover. Plants can be raised from seed sown in autumn under cover but will be variable. Useful for bonsai treatment.

Pruning Little needed apart from shortening or removing misplaced shoots in late spring or summer.

Problems Occasionally attacked by caterpillars.

Juniperus scopulorum 'Blue Heaven' (Rocky Mountain Juniper)

- Evergreen tree or shrub
- Hardiness – H2
- Care – Easy

Description Height 8ft(2.5m) at 10 years, ultimately to 20ft(6m) plus. Spread 4ft(1.2m) at 10 years, ultimately to 6ft(1.8m) plus. Somewhat variable – pyramidal to round topped. The feathery cypress-like foliage is the main attraction. It is a vivid bright silver-blue in summer dimming to grey-blue in winter. Mature plants carry blue-green berries which ripen to purple-black.

Maturity Instant foliage effects even on very young plants. Expect berrying at 15 years.

Lifespan The norm is 40 plus years of useful life.

Other varieties *J.s.* 'Skyrocket' (syn *J. virginiana* 'Skyrocket') is of similar height but about half the spread of the above. The ascending foliage is blue-green in summer and grey in winter.

Uses Probably best as accent plants among heathers or when included in conifer groupings of contrasting form and colour.

Planting Plant during spring or autumn. Allow plants an area equal to their ultimate spread plus an extra 12in(30cm) all round.

Position The foliage colour is brightest and the texture more dense and compact in open, sunny situations.

Soil Almost any free-draining light to medium soil of average fertility is suitable including those of an alkaline nature.

Propagation Take semi-ripe cuttings in early autumn and root under cover. Commercially, these varieties are grafted onto seedling rootstocks in late spring or summer.

Treatment Although tolerant of dry soils once established, keep newly set out plants well watered during the first year or two.

Pruning Little is needed apart from pruning to shape in late spring or early summer. Where a single stem tree is required, correct any tendency to forking.

Problems Occasionally attacked by juniper scale insects and by caterpillars.

Picea breweriana (Brewer's Weeping Spruce)

- Evergreen Tree
- Hardiness – H2
- Care – Easy to average

Description Height 7ft(2m) at 10 years, ultimately to 30ft(9m). Spread 2ft(60cm) at 10 years, ultimately to 15ft(4.5m). A very fine, outstanding tree of broadly conical shape and near-horizontal outstretched branches. Dark-green curtains of pendulous branchlets hang down from the branches. Individual leaves are needle-shaped with a silvery reverse. Mature trees carry cylindrical cones, green at first ripening to purple.

Maturity Although the foliage is attractive, it takes from 4–5 years before this tree makes any appreciable impact. Expect cones on trees of 35 years and older.

Lifespan In reasonable conditions a garden life of 70–80 years is the norm.

Other varieties None available readily.

Uses For maximum impact this tree needs to be seen as a specimen and is best in a large garden.

Planting Plant out in spring. Do not set closer to buildings than 30ft(9m). Allow enough room for the full spread of the tree at maturity.

Position Best in a partially shaded situation sheltered by nearby trees. Protect from north and east winds.

Soil An acid to neutral soil is needed. A cool, moist, deep, free-draining soil is preferred but this tree will grow in most soils of average fertility – alkaline soils excepted.

Propagation Graft particularly good forms in spring or summer under cover onto seed-raised rootstocks. Or, as is more usual, sow in spring under cover.

Pruning Correct any tendency to forking by removing the secondary leaders in late spring.

Problems Occasionally attacked by adelges and spruce aphids. Pollution sensitive and dislikes soot, grime and fumes.

Picea pungens 'Hoopesii'
(Colorado Spruce)

- Evergreen tree
- Hardiness – HI–2
- Care – Easy to average

Description Height 8ft(2.5m) in 10 years, ultimately to 50ft(15m). Spread 4ft(1.2m) in 10 years, ultimately to 15ft(4.5m). Of pyramidal to conical outline with dense, much-branched foliage. The needle-shaped leaves are an intense light silvery blue. Mature trees carry cones which ripen to straw colour.

Maturity Attractive foliage from day one of planting. Cone bearing begins after about 20 years.

Lifespan Calculated to be around 50 years – introduced into gardens less than 40 years ago.

Other varieties *P.p.* 'Koster' is similar in size and general habit to the above but has intense, vivid, glaucous, deep-blue foliage.

Uses First class as a specimen or planted in groups of mixed conifers in larger gardens.

Planting Set out in autumn or spring. Do not plant closer to buildings than 45ft(13.5m). Allow enough space for trees to grow to their full spread.

Position Needs full sun, an open situation and shelter from north and east winds.

Soil Grows best in acid to neutral, moist, deep, well-drained light to medium soils of average fertility. Dislikes alkaline conditions.

Propagation Graft both varieties under cover in spring or summer onto seedling rootstocks raised by sowing seeds of *P. pungens* indoors during spring.

Treatment Using a bamboo cane, support and train the leading shoot vertically for 2–3 years after planting.

Pruning Little needed. Correct any forking tendency in late spring if necessary.

Problems Adelges occasionally attack.

Pinus leucodermis (Bosnian Pine)

- Evergreen tree
- Hardiness – HI–2
- Care – Easy to average

Description Height 6ft(1.8m) in 10 years, ultimately to 30ft(9m). Spread 3ft(90cm) in 10 years, ultimately to 15ft(4.5m). This tree forms a pleasing dense foliage plant of conical outline. It becomes wider and inclined to be flat topped with age. The needle-shaped leaves are dark green and glossy. The egg-shaped rich blue cones which are produced on mature plants ripen to brown.

Maturity Of pleasing shape and foliage effect from planting. Trees start to bear cones after about 15 years.

Lifespan Expect a useful lifespan of 40 years plus.

Other varieties *P.l.* 'Satellit', height to 5ft(1.5m) at 10 years, is a promising new variety of very narrow pyramidal erect habit.

Uses Both these trees make excellent specimen

plants. *P.l.* 'Satellit' is a good accent plant amongst heathers.

Planting Preferably plant in autumn. Do not plant nearer to buildings than 25ft(7.5m). Allow *P.l.* 'Satellit' a spread of 6ft(2m). Transplants better than many other pines but still use container-grown stock.

Position Needs a sunny open site which is preferably not too exposed. Tolerant of warm, dry summer climates once established.

Soil One of the best pines for dry, thin soils. Adapts to alkaline conditions. Does well on most well-drained soils of average fertility but avoid anything over-rich.

Propagation Sow *P. leucodermis* under cover in spring. Graft *P.l.* 'Satellit' onto seedling rootstocks of *P. leucodermis* indoors in spring or summer.

Pruning Little or no pruning needed. Shorten back any damaged growths in late spring if necessary.

Problems Sometimes comes under attack from adelges and caterpillars.

Pinus nigra (Austrian Pine)

- Evergreen tree or shrub
- Hardiness – HI–2
- Care – Easy

Description Height 10ft(3m) at 10 years, ultimately to 70ft(21m) plus. Spread 5ft(1.5m) at 10 years, ultimately to 30ft(9m) plus. A dense, conical or ovoid, bushy, much-branched young tree. it becomes broader and flat topped with increasing age. The foliage comprises long needle-shaped dark-green leaves. Mature trees yield egg-shaped yellow-buff or pale grey and brown cones.

Maturity Grows quickly when young, slowing down later. Most attractive from an early age. Cone bearing usually begins within 15 years of planting.

Lifespan Expect a useful life of 40 years plus.

Other varieties *P.n.* 'Hornibrookana', a dense bushy mid-green shrub with a height and spread of about 6ft(1.8m). *P.n. maritima* (syn *P.n. calabria*

and *P.n. laricio*), Corsican pine, quicker growing than *P. nigra* reaching 80ft(24m) in height.

Uses *P. nigra* makes a good nurse crop, wind screen and barrier in coastal areas and exposed gardens. *P.n.* 'Hornibrookii' is an excellent specimen or accent plant in the small garden. *P.n. maritima* is a first-class specimen for large gardens at the coast.

Planting Plant in autumn or spring. Give each of these pines a space to grow equal to their final spread and keep *P. nigra* and *P.n. maritima* at least 50ft(15m) out from buildings. None of the pines mentioned here transplant readily after the small sapling stage.

Position Needs an open, sunny situation and preferably one that is warm or mild. Does well in coastal districts.

Soil Thrives in light to medium soils, including those of a chalky or alkaline nature, even if they are shallow and below average fertility. Must have well-drained soil however.

Propagation Raise *P. nigra* and *P.n. maritima* from seed sown in spring under cover. Graft *P.n.* 'Hornibrookii' onto seed-raised rootstocks of *P. nigra* during spring or summer indoors.

Pruning Little or no pruning needed. Shorten back any damaged growths in late spring if necessary.

Problems Sometimes comes under attack from adelges and caterpillars.

Pinus sylvestris (Scots Pine)

- Evergreen tree
- Hardiness – HI
- Care – Easy

Description Height 15ft(4.5m) in 10 years, ultimately to 60ft(18m). Spread 5ft(1.5m) in 10 years, ultimately to 20ft(6m). A bushy, conical, dense foliaged young tree. Becomes gaunt and flat topped with age. A high crown and exposed attractive reddish-brown trunk are characteristic. The foliage comprises aromatic blue-green or grey-green needles. The cones ripen to pale brown.

Fig 105 Pinus sylvestris (Scots pine). This specimen is more compact than many – Scots pines come in many forms.

Maturity Moderately quick growing when young and slow in old age. Very pleasing foliage from planting out, cones are produced on trees of 10 years and over.

Lifespan Picturesque trees of 100 years old can occasionally be found.

Other varieties Two of the best varieties for small to medium sized gardens are *P.s.* 'Aurea', height to 30ft(9m), spread 10ft(3m), slow growing with golden winter foliage, and *P.s.* 'Fastigiata' height to 15ft(4.5m), spread 4ft(1.2m), a rare narrow columnar form with grey-green foliage.

Uses *P. sylvestris* is a specimen tree for large gardens or for group planting with conifers. Sometimes used as a temporary nurse crop for azaleas and rhododendrons. The two varieties mentioned make excellent specimen trees and look good as accent plants in beds or borders with heathers and conifers in the smaller garden.

Planting Plant in autumn or spring. Keep these trees at a distance from buildings equal to their ultimate height.

Position Needs a sunny, open situation that is not too exposed. *P.s.* 'Aurea' and *P.s.* 'Fastigiata' require shelter and adapt well to areas with warm, dry climates.

Soil Although these trees prefer mildly acid to neutral conditions they will adapt to moderately alkaline soils. A light to medium well-drained soil which is not over-rich, and of average or slightly below average fertility is suitable.

Propagation Increase *P. sylvestris* by sowing indoors during spring. *P.s.* 'Aurea' and *P.s.* 'Fastigiata' are grafted under cover onto seed-raised rootstocks of *P. sylvestris* also in spring.

Treatment Protect *P.s.* 'Aurea' and *P.s.* 'Fastigiata' from wind during their first winter unless in a very favoured garden.

Pruning Little or no pruning needed. Shorten back any damaged shoots in late spring if necessary.

Problems Sometimes comes under attack from adelgids and caterpillars.

Taxus baccata (Yew)

- Evergreen tree or shrub
- Hardiness – H1
- Care – Easy to demanding

Description Height 6ft(1.8m) at 10 years, ultimately to 35ft(10.5m). Spread 8ft(2.5m) at 10 years, ultimately to 25ft(7.5m). A broadly conical, bushy tree or shrub, becoming more rounded or domed with increasing age. The dark-green leaves are needle-like and poisonous to grazing animals. Female plants produce small bright red berry-like fruits when mature.

Maturity These slow-growing plants may take 2–3 years before making any appreciable visual impact but fruiting does not normally begin for a number of years.

Lifespan Yew is one of the longest lived of any garden plants.

Other varieties *T.b.* 'Fastigiata' (Irish yew)

when allowed to grow unrestricted will make a dark-green column or spire up to 20ft(6m) in height. *T.b.* 'Standishii', a slow-growing columnar variety with golden foliage and growing to about 12ft(3.5m) tall.

Uses *T. baccata* is versatile with many uses including specimen planting, as hedging, as a backdrop, as clipped topiary, and to provide shelter and screening. *T.b.* 'Fastigiata' and *T.b.* 'Standishii' make excellent specimens as well as accent plants in beds and borders among conifers or heathers. Good for use in pairs to frame views and doorways.

Planting Plant in autumn, spring or during mild spells in winter. Do not allow tree forms of *T. baccata* to grow nearer to buildings than 20ft(6m). Space hedging plants about 20in(50cm) apart.

Position Grows well in sun or partial shade. *T.b.* 'Standishii' colours better in sun.

Soil Adapts to almost any soil of average fertility including those of a light sandy, heavy or alkaline nature.

Propagation Sow *T. baccata* in October under cover. Alternatively, take semi-ripe cuttings in September and root indoors.

Pruning Pruning should be carried out in late spring or summer. Shorten straggly shoots and clip in the sides of hedges and topiary but do not remove the tops until the required height is reached.

Problems Yew scale can be a problem.

Thuja occidentalis 'Smaragd'
(American Arbor–Vitae, Arbor-Vitae)

- Evergreen tree or shrub
- Hardiness – H2
- Care – Easy to average

Description Height 8ft(2.5m) in 10 years, ultimately to 25ft(7.5m) plus. Spread 2½ft(75cm) at 10 years, ultimately to 8ft(2.5m). A moderate- to slow-growing pyramidal or conical narrow tree or shrub with bright emerald-green cypress-like foliage. Mature plants bear small globular cones of yellow ripening to brown.

Maturity Attractive foliage right from planting out; cone bearing starts in 8–10 years.

Lifespan A garden life of 25 years plus is usual.

Other varieties *T.o.* 'Europe Gold', a vivid golden foliaged version of the above.

Uses Good as specimens, as pairs to frame views, as accent plants amongst heathers, for grouping midst conifers, for hedging and screening, and for container use.

Planting Plant in spring or autumn. Do not direct plant closer to buildings than 20ft(6m). Allow plants space to grow equivalent to their spread.

Position Needs sun. Avoid very exposed sites.

Soil Flourishes in any free-draining, moist soil of average fertility including those of an alkaline or heavy nature. Use standard soil-based potting compost for containers.

Propagation Take semi-ripe or green cuttings in early autumn and root under cover.

Pruning Minimal pruning, apart from shortening back straggly shoots and cutting out surplus leaders where forking occurs. Unless multi-stemmed trees are the aim leave only one main stem.

Problems Once established, trouble free.

Thuja plicata 'Atrovirens' (Western Red Cedar)

- Evergreen tree
- Hardiness – H2
- Care – Easy to average

Description Height 20ft(6m) at 10 years, ultimately to 70ft(21m) plus. Spread 7ft(2m) at 10 years ultimately to 20ft(6m). Quickly grows into a tall conical or pyramidal tree. It has dense, semi-pendulous, bright green, vigorous, cypress-like foliage which droops at the branch tips. Mature trees bear small brown globular cones.

Maturity The foliage is an altogether pleasing feature from the start. Cones are produced on 10-year-old trees.

Fig 106 Thuja plicata 'Aurea'. Makes a good, quick-growing specimen tree. But because it stands clipping in moderation it can also be used as hedging.

Planting Plant in autumn or spring. Avoid planting closer to buildings than 50ft(15m) unless the height is restricted as with hedging. Plant hedging 2–2½ft(60–75cm) apart. Give specimens and group-planted conifers a space equal to their final spread.

Position Golden varieties need sun, others will tolerate partial shade. Avoid very exposed sites.

Soil Flourishes in any well-drained moist soil of average fertility including those of an alkaline or heavy nature. Use standard soil-based potting compost for containers.

Propagation Take semi-ripe or green cuttings in early autumn and root under cover.

Pruning Minimal, apart from shortening back straggly shoots and cutting out surplus leaders where forking occurs. Unless multi-stemmed trees are the aim leave only one main stem.

Problems Once established, trouble free.

DWARF AND SLOW-GROWING CONIFERS

Abies balsamea 'Hudsonia' (Balsam Fir)

- Evergreen shrub
- Hardiness – H2
- Care – Easy

Description Height 12in(30cm) at 10 years ultimately to 3ft(90cm). Spread 20in(50cm) at 10 years, ultimately to 4ft(1.2m) A neat, rounded, dense bushy shrub grown for its foliage and form. The short needle-like leaves are dark green with pale reverse. Cones are not a feature.

Maturity This very slow-growing shrub is attractive from an early age.

Lifespan A useful garden life of 30 years is common.

Other varieties *A.b.* 'Nana' is very similar to above but more blue-green. *A.b.* 'Prostrata' is again similar but more grey-green.

Uses Valuable in the rock garden, in raised beds, as a container plant, and in beds and

Lifespan Long lived – will survive upwards of 100 years.

Other varieties *T.p.* 'Aurea', a golden form of the above of similar size and habit. *T.p.* 'Fastigiata', a narrower version. *T.* 'Zebrina', an attractive conical quick-growing tree with bright gold bands among the green, similar size to *T.p.* 'Atrovirens'.

Uses All make excellent specimens, are fine for framing views as well as for hedging, screening and container work. They provide a good background for shrub beds and borders. They are invaluable for group planting with other conifers of contrasting colours.

Fig 107 Abies balsamea 'Nana' — a useful, tiny, globose conifer which adapts well to sun or shade.

borders with other dwarf conifers and heathers.

Planting Preferably plant in spring. An initial minimum area equivalent to a 20in(50cm) spread is adequate for the first 10 years.

Position Grows well in sun or partial shade in an open situation provided it is not too exposed.

Soil Prefers a light to medium well-drained, moist, acid to neutral soil. Will adapt to slightly alkaline conditions. Use soil-based potting compost in containers.

Propagation Graft under cover in spring onto seed raised rootstocks grown from seed of *A. balsamea* sown indoors during spring.

Treatment Use soft rainwater to spray over the foliage in the evenings during warm, dry weather to discourage red spider mite.

Pruning Not normally needed. If necessary shorten straggly shoots in late spring.

Problems Occasionally attacked by adelges.

Chamaecyparis lawsoniana 'Aurea Densa' (Lawson's Cypress)

- Evergreen shrub
- Hardiness – HI–2
- Care – Easy

Description Height 12in(30cm) in 10 years, ultimately to 20in(50cm). Spread 12in(30cm) in 10 years, ultimately to 20in(50cm). A compact, dense, much-branched dome-shaped dwarf shrub. Its chief attraction is the bright golden foliage which retains colour year round. Cones are normally absent.

Maturity A colourful and interesting very slow-growing conifer gardenworthy from planting time.

Lifespan With care a useful garden life of 30 years plus should be attainable.

Other varieties *C.l.* 'Ellwood Pillar', height to 3ft(90cm) in 10 years, a delightful grey-green slender column of close-knit foliage. *C.l.* 'Gnome', height ultimately 20in(50cm), a dark-green bushy globe. *C.l.* 'Minima Aurea', height to 20in(50cm) in 10 years, a charming close-textured pyramid of gold. *C.l.* 'Minima Glauca', height ultimately 3ft(90cm), a dense ball of blue-grey and green.

Uses All are splendid selections for raised beds, rock gardens and containers, as well as for planting among heathers in beds and borders and group plantings of mixed dwarf conifers.

Fig 108 Chamaecyparis lawsoniana 'Minima Aurea' — a versatile, useful conifer suitable for container growing or direct planting in the border or rock garden. Likes sun.

Planting Preferably plant in spring. To show off these gems to advantage, allow each plant an area equal to double its spread.

Position Does best in an open, sunny situation which is not too exposed. Needs shelter from north and east winds and early morning sun.

Soil Any good well-drained, moist soil of fair to above average fertility should suit including those of an alkaline or heavy nature. Soil-based potting compost is best for containers.

Propagation Take semi-ripe cuttings in early autumn and root under cover.

Pruning Shorten back straggly or damaged shoots in late spring or early summer.

Problems Generally trouble free.

Chamaecyparis obtusa 'Nana Gracilis' (Hinoki Cypress)

- Evergreen shrub
- Hardiness – H2–3
- Care – Easy to average

Description Height 2ft(60cm) at 10 years, ultimately to 5ft(1.5m). Spread 2ft(60cm) at 10 years, ultimately to 5ft(1.5m). A very distinctive, dense, bushy conical mound. The foliage is rich green and arranged in curious fan-shaped sprays. Cones are not a feature.

Maturity This very slow-growing conifer is visually pleasing from the day of planting.

Lifespan When reasonably well cared for, will last for 60 years plus.

Other varieties *C.o.* 'Nana Lutea', a slightly narrower, pyramidal golden form of the above. *C.o.* 'Fernspray Gold', of similar size at 10 years but ultimately probably larger and forms a rounded mound of feathery bright green and gold.

Uses These varieties make splendid selections for raised beds, rock gardens and containers. Good for planting amongst heathers in beds and borders as well as for group plantings of mixed dwarf conifers.

Planting Preferably plant in spring. To display these rather special plants to advantage, allow each an area equal to double its spread.

Position Does best in an open, sunny situation which is not too exposed. Needs shelter from north and east winds and early morning sun.

Soil Best on acid to neutral soil. Otherwise any good, well-drained, moist soil of fair to above average fertility should suit including those inclined to be heavy. Use soil-based potting compost in containers.

Propagation Take semi-ripe cuttings in early autumn and root under cover.

Pruning Shorten back straggly or damaged shoots in late spring or early summer.

Problems Generally trouble free.

Chamaecyparis pisifera 'Nana' (Sawara Cypress)

- Evergreen shrub
- Hardiness – H2–3
- Care – Easy to average

Description Height 8in(20cm) at 10 years, ultimately to 18in(45cm). Spread 12in(30cm) at 10 years, ultimately to 24in(60cm). A fairly neat and compact bun-shaped bush with dark-green much-branched foliage. Normally non-cone bearing.

Maturity The foliage is interesting from the outset. This is a very slow-growing shrub, putting on about 1in(3cm) per year.

Lifespan Expect a garden life of 25 years plus.

Other varieties *C.p.* 'Nana Aurea' is a golden foliaged replica of the above.

Uses Eminently suitable for rock garden, raised bed, container work and for planting with mixed dwarf conifers in beds and borders.

Planting Plant in spring. Allow each plant a minimum area of about 16in(40cm) square.

Position Both these shrubs grow well in open sunny sites but *C.p.* 'Nana' can adapt to partial light shade. Needs shelter from wind and early morning sun.

Soil Needs an acid to neutral, moist, well-drained light to medium soil of average fertility. Use soil-based potting compost for containers.

Propagation Take semi-ripe cuttings in early autumn and root under cover.

Fig 109 Chamaecyparis obtusa *'Nana Aurea'* *– a narrow columnar form which fits into little space.*

Pruning Shorten back any straggly or damaged shoots in late spring or early summer.
Pruning Generally trouble free.

Chamaecyparis thyoides 'Andeleyensis Nana' (White Cypress)

- Evergreen shrub
- Hardiness – H2–3
- Care – Easy

Description Height 20in(50cm) in 10 years, ultimately to 3ft(90cm). Spread 20in(50cm) in 10 years, ultimately to 3ft(90cm). Somewhat variable in habit ranging from broadly conical to dense, flat topped and bushy. The foliage is rich green and feathery. Cones are usually absent.

Maturity A useful and interesting addition from the time of planting.
Lifespan Anticipate a useful garden life of at least 30 years.
Other varieties *C.t.* 'Ericoides', similar size to the above, of conical habit with sea-green soft bushy foliage in summer, turning soft bronze-purple in winter. *C.t.* 'Rubicon', slightly larger than the above, the close-textured bronze summer foliage becomes wine-red in winter.
Uses Excellent as a raised bed and rock garden conifer. Good in containers and in mixed dwarf conifer beds and borders. Looks well with compact heathers.
Planting Ideally plant in spring. Allow each plant a minimum area of 18in(45cm).
Position Adapts to sun or partial shade. Prefers an open, sheltered site with protection from north and east winds.
Soil Needs an acid to neutral moist soil of average fertility. Although it enjoys moister ground than many conifers it must be well drained.
Propagation Take semi-ripe cuttings in early autumn and root under cover.
Pruning Shorten back straggly or damaged shoots in late spring or early summer.
Problems Generally trouble free.

Cryptomeria japonica 'Compressa' (Japanese Cedar)

- Evergreen shrub
- Hardiness – H2–3
- Care – Easy to average

Description Height 16in(40cm) in 10 years, ultimately to 3ft(90cm). Spread 16in(40cm) in 10 years, ultimately to 3ft(90cm). A flat-topped or domed, globe-shaped shrub much branched yet compact. Grown for its foliage and form. The summer foliage is bronze-green, turning reddish purple in winter. Cones are scarce or absent.
Maturity The instant foliage effects of this very slow-growing conifer make it a useful addition right from planting time.

Lifespan In congenial surroundings expect a useful life of 40 years plus.

Other varieties *C.j.* 'Vilmoriniana', almost a mirror model of the above for size and colour but is neater and more rounded with a freer form. *C.j.* 'Spiralis', height and spread to 2ft(60cm) at 10 years. The foliage is bright green. The leaves twist curiously around the stems hence its popular name of granny's ringlets.

Uses Valuable plants for raised beds, rock gardens, including beds and borders of mixed dwarf conifers and for container work.

Planting Ideally plant in spring or alternatively in autumn on light sandy soils in mild climate areas. Allow each plant a minimum space of 16in(40cm) square initially.

Position A sunny sheltered spot is excellent or a west-facing, partially shaded aspect makes a good alternative. Although these conifers adapt to light shade the foliage colour is inferior and the plants become less compact.

Soil An acid, deep, moist, cool, well-drained soil is a must for best results. The ground should be of a good average level of fertility.

Propagation Take semi-ripe cuttings in early autumn and root under cover.

Treatment Protect young plants from wind and frost especially in their first winter. Winter mulch. Particularly sensitive to weed competition and dryness – keep weed-free and watered throughout their first year.

Pruning Minimal. Shorten any damaged or straggly shoots in late spring or summer.

Problems Trouble free provided its cultural needs are met.

Juniperus communis 'Compressa' (Juniper)

- Evergreen shrub
- Hardiness – H1–2
- Care – Easy to average

Description Height 16in(40cm) at 10 years, ultimately to 2½ft(75cm). Spread 6in(15cm) at 10 years, ultimately to 8in(20cm). Grows into a dense, narrow pyramid or column of close-knit foliage and neat appearance. The foliage is a pleasant grey-green enlivened by light green new tip growths in late spring. Non-berrying.

Maturity Very slow growing but of great charm and interest from the instant it is planted.

Lifespan Normally long lived – expect a life of 60 years plus.

Other varieties *J.c.* 'Depressa Aurea', height to 16in(40cm), spread 4ft(1.2m) at 10 years, a superb low growing, spreading ground cover plant. Brilliant yellow new growths enliven the branches each spring turning to pale gold and bronze in winter.

Uses *J.c.* 'Compressa' makes an outstanding focal point in a rock garden, raised bed or container used on its own with rock plants or in groups of two, three or more. *J.c.* 'Depressa Aurea' is first class as a specimen in a rock garden or at the waterside and when used as ground cover.

Planting Plant in autumn or spring. Allow each *J.c.* 'Compressa' an area of 12in(30cm) square, make it 4ft(1.2m) square for specimen *J.c.* 'Depressa Aurea' or one plant per sq yd(m) for ground cover.

Position *J.c.* 'Compressa' does best in an open, sunny site sheltered from freezing conditions in winter but it will adapt to partial shade. *J.c.* 'Depressa Aurea' needs sun and shelter to colour thoroughly.

Soil Grows well in almost any well-drained soil of average fertility including those of an alkaline or heavy nature. Use soil-based potting compost in containers.

Propagation Take semi-ripe cuttings of about 3in(8cm) in length with a heel in early autumn, and root under cover.

Treatment With ground cover plantings pay special attention to keeping the land weed-free.

Pruning Shorten straggly or damaged growths in late spring or summer and shorten the tips of ground cover to restrict to the allotted area.

Problems Liable to attack by juniper scale insects and by caterpillars.

Juniperus horizontalis 'Blue Chip' (syn 'Blue Moon') (Creeping Juniper)

- Evergreen shrub
- Hardiness – HI–2
- Care – Easy to average

Description Height 8in(20cm) at 10 years, ultimately to 16in(40cm). Spread 4ft(1.2m) at 10 years ultimately to indefinite. A mat-forming variety with long procumbent or ground-hugging branches which put down roots as they grow. Long-established plants form a dense, weed-smothering mat up to 16in(40cm) or more in depth. Non-fruiting.

Maturity Although moderate to quick growing it takes 2 or 3 years for complete ground cover subject to correct spacing and good cultivations.

Lifespan A life of 30 years plus is the norm.

Other varieties *J.h.* 'Glauca' similar in habit to the above but slightly stronger growing and has steel-blue foliage. *J.h.* 'Prince of Wales' is less vigorous than *J.h.* 'Blue Chip' and its bright green foliage of summer becomes tinged purple-brown in winter.

Uses Essentially ground cover plants. But in the case of *J.h.* 'Prince of Wales', effective as underplanting.

Planting Plant in autumn or spring. Allow one plant per sq yd(m) for both ground cover and underplanting. Set out container-raised plants in completely weed-free ground. Initial weed control among ground cover is essential but can be tricky.

Position Best in open sunny situations. *J.h.* 'Prince of Wales' will adapt to partial shade.

Soil Thrives in almost any well-drained soil of average fertility including those of an alkaline or heavy nature.

Propagation Take semi-ripe cuttings in early autumn, 3in(8cm) long with a heel and root under cover.

Treatment Pay special attention to keeping the land weed-free.

Pruning Shorten straggly or damaged growths in late spring or summer and shorten the tips of ground cover to restrict to allotted area.

Problems Liable to attack by juniper scale insects and by caterpillars.

Juniperus x media 'Old Gold' (Hybrid Juniper)

- Evergreen shrub
- Hardiness – HI–2
- Care – Easy to average

Description Height 3ft(90cm) at 10 years, ultimately to 4ft(1.2m). Spread 4ft(1.2m) at 10 years, ultimately to 10ft(3m). A vase-shaped or flat-topped spreading shrub with dense drooping tipped foliage. The dark-green and old gold-mix of colourings persist year round. Berries are not a feature.

Maturity The interesting foliage and outline contribute usefully from the day they are planted out.

Lifespan A fairly recent introduction but a life of 40 years should be possible.

Fig 110 Juniperus x media 'Sulphur Spray' makes a useful small shrub on most soils including alkaline.

Other varieties *J. x m.* 'Mint Julep', height 2½ft(75cm), spread 4ft(1.2m) at 10 years. A fairly recent introduction, flat-topped, semi-prostrate arching branches and mint-green foliage. *J. x m.* 'Sulphur Spray' of similar size and shape to *J. x m.* 'Mint Julep' with creamy white and green colourings.

Uses Makes a splendid specimen on its own, good as an accent plant amongst heathers and dwarf conifers and is first rate as a focal point and corner plant.

Planting Plant in autumn or spring. Allow each shrub a minimum 4ft(1.2m) spread at planting time.

Position Needs a sunny situation preferably warm and sheltered from high winds. *J. x m.* 'Mint Julep' adapts to partial shade.

Soil Grows well in most soils of average fertility, moist as well as dry, and including those inclined to be alkaline.

Propagation Take semi-ripe heel cuttings in early autumn and root under cover.

Pruning Shorten straggly or damaged growths in late spring or summer. If required shrubs can be restricted to 10-year spread by careful pruning.

Problems Liable to attack by juniper scale insects and by caterpillars.

Juniperus squamata 'Blue Star'
(Juniper)

- Evergreen shrub
- Hardiness – H2
- Care – Average

Description Height 12in(30cm) at 10 years, ultimately to 20in(50cm). Spread 18in(45cm) at 10 years, ultimately to 24in(60cm). A small compact, bushy, rounded shrub with dense foliage of a bright steel blue. The colour is retained well year round. Berries are rarely produced.

Maturity Although slow growing adds a bright touch of colour, even when newly planted.

Lifespan Looks good for about 15 years, then gets rather untidy.

Other varieties *J.s.* 'Blue Carpet', height 12in(30cm), spread 5ft(1.5m) at 10 years, a prostrate carpeting shrub.

Uses *J.s.* 'Blue Star' is first class as an accent plant in rock garden, raised bed and border. *J.s.* 'Blue Carpet' is a very fine ground cover subject.

Planting Plant in autumn or spring. Allow each *J.s.* 'Blue Star' a minimum 16in(40cm) spread. Set one plant per sq yd(m) in the case of *J.s.* 'Blue Carpet'.

Position Needs a sunny, open situation protected from strong wind.

Soil Seems to prefer an acid to neutral well-drained light to medium soil of average or slightly below average fertility.

Propagation Take semi-ripe heel cuttings in early autumn and root under cover.

Treatment Keep both these conifers clear of any other plants or weeds which will compete for light or air.

Pruning Minimal. Shorten any untidy or straggly growths in late spring. Similarly shorten the tips of *J.s.* 'Blue Carpet' to restrict the spread if necessary.

Problems Generally trouble free.

Picea glauca albertiana 'Conica' (syn P.a. 'Albertiana Conica') (White Spruce)

- Evergreen shrub
- Hardiness – H2
- Care – Average

Description Height 2½ft(75cm) at 10 years, ultimately to 6ft(1.8m). Spread 12in(30cm) at 10 years, ultimately to 4ft(1.2m). Forms a perfect cone of dense, close-knit foliage, one of the very best dwarf conifers in cultivation. Each spring new needle-like leaves open bright green, paling to resemble the older foliage by late summer. Insignificant small rounded brown cones are produced on mature plants.

Maturity A very slow growing and beautiful conifer from planting out time onwards. Cones are not normally produced for many years.

Fig III Juniperus squamata *'Blue Star' — one of the most striking, steely-blue conifers in cultivation, but it must have sun.*

Lifespan With good cultivations will last for 70 years plus.

Other varieties *P.g.* 'Alberta Globe', a rounded mid-green mound about 18in(45cm) high at 10 years. It has bright green spring foliage. *P.g.* 'Laurin' is a slower growing miniature replica of *P.g.a.* 'Conica'.

Uses Excellent in rock gardens and raised beds, in sinks and trough gardens, in patio beds, in conifer borders, and in heather beds.

Planting Plant out in spring unless conditions are near perfect, when autumn planting is an alternative. Allow each plant a minimum 18in(45cm) spread at planting time with planned space for long-term growth.

Position At their best in a moist climate. Suits sun or partial shade but needs shelter from cold or drying winds.

Soil Requires an acid to neutral soil. Preferably one which is moist, well-drained and of good average fertility. Use lime-free soil-based potting compost in containers.

Propagation Graft indoors during spring or summer onto seed-raised rootstocks and raise by sowing *P. glauca* under cover during spring.

Treatment In warm, dry weather spray over the foliage in the evenings using soft clean rainwater. This is to discourage red spider mite.

Pruning Carry out any essential shortening of shoots in summer but keep to a minimum.

Problems Liable to attack by pests such as adelges, aphid and red spider mite.

Picea mariana 'Nana' (Black Spruce)

- Evergreen shrub
- Hardiness – HI–2
- Care – Easy to average

Description Height 6in(15cm) at 10 years, ultimately to 20in(50cm). Spread 10in(25cm) at 10 years, ultimately to 2½ft(75cm). Makes a small, compact, bun-shaped shrub which is characteristically wider than tall. The tips of new spring shoots are blue-green, turning to grey-green by late summer. Cones are rare.

Maturity Very slow growing but attractive at all stages.

Lifespan When well cared for a life of 35 years plus can be expected.

Other varieties This is the only true dwarf variety. *P.m.* 'Aureovariegata' is dwarf up to about 15 years.

Uses Excellent in raised beds and in the rock garden. Especially valuable in containers.

Planting Plant in spring. Allow each plant a minimum 12in(30cm) space when planting with planned room allocation for ultimate spread.

Position Will adapt to sun or partial shade but needs to be sheltered from wind.

Soil Requires acid to neutral, cool, moist, well-drained soil of average fertility. Use lime-free soil-based potting compost in containers.

Propagation Pin down layers in spring or autumn. It will take them 2 years to root and be ready to lift.

Treatment Avoid overcrowding by more vigorous neighbours.

Pruning Not necessary as a rule.

Problems Subject to occasional attacks by adelges and aphids.

Picea pungens 'Prostrata' (Colorado Spruce)

- Evergreen shrub
- Hardiness – H2
- Care – Average

Description Height 12in(30cm) at 10 years. Spread 2½ft(75cm) at 10 years. Forms a low growing, prostrate shrub. Occasionally it throws up a vigorous, vertical stem. The needle-like foliage is a pleasing glaucous blue, noticeably bluer in spring and greying during winter. The leaves have a pale reverse. Cones are seldom, if ever, produced.

Maturity Of interest from the outset.

Lifespan Relatively short lived with a useful garden life of 15 years or so at which time the plants become jaded and untidy.

Other varieties *P.p.* 'Globosa', height and span up to about 2ft(60cm). Forms a flat-topped globular bush with bright silver-blue spring foliage dulling to a more grey-silver during winter.

Uses Both these shrubs are excellent in raised beds and in rock gardens. *P.p.* 'Prostrata' makes an eyecatching accent plant amongst heathers and looks good in mixed dwarf conifer beds. *P.p.* 'Globosa' is a natural for container growing.

Planting Best planted in spring. Allow both varieties a minimum 2ft(60cm) spread.

Position Needs a sunny, open situation sheltered from cold or drying winds.

Soil Requires acid to neutral, cool, moist, well-drained soil of average fertility. Use lime-free soil-based potting compost in containers.

Propagation Graft during spring or summer indoors onto seed-raised rootstocks. Grow these by sowing *P. pungens* under cover during spring.

Treatment Avoid overcrowding with more vigorous plants.

Pruning Minimal. But with *P.p.* 'Prostrata' remove any vertical upward-growing shoots during summer in order to retain the prostrate character of this variety.

Problems Liable to attack by adelges and aphids.

Pinus mugo 'Ophir' (Mountain Pine)

- Evergreen shrub
- Hardiness – HI–2
- Care – Easy

Description Height 16in(40cm) at 10 years, ultimately to 3ft(90cm). Spread 24in(60cm) at 10 years, ultimately to 7ft(2m). A fairly compact, domed or rounded bush which is wider than high. The foliage is the chief attraction with gold-tipped dark-green long pine needles. They turn to gold in winter to lighten up the whole plant. Cones are usually absent.

Maturity Eyecatching from the start.

Lifespan Given reasonable cultivation a useful garden life of 50 years plus should be attainable.

Other varieties *P.m.* 'Mops', a rounded grey-green bush of like height and reduced spread.

Uses A first-rate rock garden plant; looks well planted around with heathers, and is valuable in mixed groupings of dwarf conifers of contrasting texture, colour and shape.

Planting Plant in autumn or spring. Give each shrub a minimum 3ft(90cm) spread with anticipated allowance for extra space after 10 years. Dislikes root disturbance so use container-grown plants.

Position Needs a sunny, open site. Ensure a degree of shelter for the golden variety. *P.c.* 'Mops' will adapt to partial shade.

Soil Grows well in most light to medium well-drained soils of average fertility including those of an alkaline nature.

Propagation Graft both varieties onto seed-raised rootstocks under cover in spring or summer. Grow rootstocks from seed of *P. mugo*, sown indoors in spring.

Treatment Essential to keep weed-free until a good blanket of foliage is produced.

Pruning Not as a rule called for.

Problems Liable to occasional attacks by adelges and caterpillars.

Pinus strobus 'Nana' (Weymouth Pine)

- Evergreen shrub
- Hardiness – H3
- Care – Easy to average

Description Height 3ft(90cm) at 10 years, ultimately to 5ft(1.5m). Spread 3½ft(100cm) at 10 years, ultimately to 7ft(2m). Variable, ranging from dense, compact, rounded bushes with branches completely hidden from view by foliage to those of a sparsely foliaged nature and open habit. The glaucous-blue needles are arranged in tufts of five. Cones are not normally a feature.

Maturity Attractive at any age.

Lifespan Give good cultivations should have a useful garden life of 40 years plus.

Other varieties *P.s.* 'Reinhaus' is a smaller form of the above with a height and spread of up to 2ft(60cm) in 10 years.

Uses Excellent as specimens, as rock garden plants, as accent plants among heathers, and for inclusion in mixed conifer groupings. A good coastal conifer but not suited to town pollution.

Planting Plant in autumn. Allow a minimum initial spacing equal to spread at 10 years with anticipated provision for more room later on.

Position Enjoys the climate of the south coast. Needs a warm, sunny site, sheltered from cold or freezing winds especially those from the north or east.

Soil Requires acid to neutral soil, well drained and light to medium in texture.

Propagation Graft both varieties onto seed-raised rootstocks of *P. strobus* under cover in spring or summer. Grow rootstocks from seed sown indoors in spring.

Pruning Not normally required. Do any essential shortening of damaged shoots in early summer.

Problems Liable to attack by adelges and by white rust disease.

Pinus sylvestris 'Beavronensis' (Scots Pine)

- Evergreen shrub
- Hardiness – H1–2
- Care – Easy to average

Description Height 2ft(60cm) at 10 years, ultimately to 3ft(90cm). Spread 2ft(60cm) at 10 years, ultimately to 3ft(90cm). Makes a pleasing, dome-shaped bush in the early years, developing a thick, flat-topped crown with sparcely branched or bare base with age. This is in fact a veritable miniature Scots pine with blue-grey needles. Cones are rarely produced.

Maturity This typical pine-in-miniature has much to contribute from an early age.

Lifespan Expect a useful garden life of 40 years plus.

Other varieties *P.s.* 'Doone Valley', conical or pyramidal in outline, otherwise similar to above as regards foliage and colour.

Uses Excellent in the rock garden and in raised alpine beds as well as being first class for container work. Looks good when set out in mixed beds of dwarf conifers.

Planting Preferably plant in autumn. Allow each shrub at least 2½ft(75cm) spread at planting time bearing in mind more space may be needed at a later date.

Position Best in open sunny situations sheltered from the full force of prevailing winds. Where practical, set at eye height to gain maximum visual impact.

Soil Grows well in acid to netural, light to medium well-drained soil of average or even below average fertility. Lime-free soil-based potting compost is needed for containers.

Propagation Both these varieties are grafted onto seed-raised rootstocks of *P. sylvestris* and kept indoors until the grafts have taken. Grow rootstocks from seed sown undercover in spring.

Pruning Not as a rule necessary. On shrubs of over 10 years old it helps to remove the odd lower branch in summer which exposes stems to view and lets in light and air.

Problems Occasionally comes under attack from adelges.

Taxus baccata 'Repens Aurea'
(Yew)

- Evergreen shrub
- Hardiness – H1
- Care – Easy to average

Description Height 18in(45cm) at 10 years,

ultimately to 20in(60cm). Spread 3ft(90cm) at 10 years, ultimately to 7ft(2m). A prostrate, spreading shrub which is grown primarily for its foliage. The leaves are golden yellow, brightest in summer and greening in winter. This is a female variety which when pollinated will produce red berry-like fruits of currant size.

Maturity Attractive at any age, fruiting begins within 10 years of planting.

Lifespan Very long lived – well beyond the 100-year mark.

Other varieties *T.b.* 'Repandens' is a dark-green, stronger growing form of the above eventually reaching 2ft(60cm) high by 15ft(4.5m) wide if unchecked. This is another female berrying variety.

Uses Good as a specimen, as ground cover, and in beds and borders.

Planting Plant anytime between autumn and spring during mild spells. Allow specimen plants an area of up to 5ft(1.5m) across reducing to 4ft(1.2m) for ground cover. When planting out aim to include at least one male to four female plants to ensure free berrying.

Position Best in full sun in open but not too draughty or exposed situations. The golden variety loses colour in the shade.

Soil Grows well in most soils that are well drained and of average fertility including those of a chalky or heavy nature. Slightly alkaline conditions are preferred.

Propagation Take semi-ripe cuttings in early autumn and root under cover.

Treatment Syringe the foliage in the evenings with clean water during warm dry weather.

Pruning In late spring or summer, shorten straggly shoots and clip as necessary to contain shrubs within their allotted space.

Problems Occasionally attacked by yew scale.

Thuja occidentalis 'Rheingold'
(American Arbor-Vitae White Cedar)

- Evergreen shrub
- Hardiness – H2–3
- Care – Average

Description Height 4ft(1.2m) at 10 years, ultimately to 7ft(2m) but variable. Spread 2½ft(75cm) at 10 years, ultimately to 5ft(1.5m) but variable. Variable in shape ranging from rounded to conical with bushy, dense, feathery foliage. The ultimate size is also unpredictable ranging from about 5ft(1.5m) in height up to 10ft(3m) in favourable surroundings. The foliage takes on lovely burnished gold and copper shadings in summer turning darker in winter. Cones are usually absent.

Maturity This shrub has great interest and appeal from planting time onwards.

Lifespan Relatively short lived, ranging from 10–12 years on dry, alkaline soils to 25 years on moist, acid soils.

Other varieties T.o. 'Danica', an attractive rounded bush of about 16in(40cm) high in 10 years. The foliage is deep green in summer turning to bronze shadings in winter. T.o. 'Sunkist' similar to T.o. 'Danica' but of bright golden yellow.

Uses Excellent as specimens and accent plants and good in rock gardens and in beds of mixed conifers. T.o. 'Danica' and T.o. 'Sunkist' are good in raised alpine beds, in containers as well as in the rock garden.

Planting Preferably plant in spring. Allow T.o. 'Reingold' a minimum 4ft(1.2m) spread and allow 2½ft(75cm) for the other two varieties. Make provision for more space at maturity.

Position Best in an open, sunny site sheltered from cold winds. T.o. 'Danica' will adapt to partial light shade.

Soil Prefers an acid to neutral, moist, well-drained soil of good average fertility. Dislikes hot, shallow, dry, alkaline conditions. Use lime-free soil-based potting compost in containers.

Propagation Take semi-ripe cuttings in early autumn and root under cover.

Treatment Essential to keep weed-free, well watered and mulched in the early years after planting. Take steps to prevent overcrowding. And if Thuja blight strikes, spray the foliage with fungicide at the earliest opportunity in dull calm weather.

Pruning Clip or shorten back young shoots by no more than a third of the young growth in late spring or summer.

Problems Liable to attack by Thuja blight.

Thuja orientalis 'Aurea Nana' (Chinese Arbor-vitae)

- Evergreen shrub
- Hardiness – H3
- Care – Easy to average

Description Height 2ft(60cm) in 10 years, ultimately to 2½ft(75cm). Spread 12in(30cm) in

Fig 112 Thuja orientalis 'Aurea Nana' – an oval– shaped, neat, attractive, popularly grown conifer which does best in sun.

10 years, ultimately to 2ft(60cm). A neat, symmetrical, oval bush, of dense compact foliage comprising vertically arranged sprays. The foliage is golden yellow and green in summer, becoming bronze-green in winter. Cones are normally absent.

Maturity A charming conifer at any age.

Lifespan Relatively short lived – expect a useful life of about 15–20 years.

Other varieties *T.o.* 'Rosedalis', of similar size and shape to above with delightful feathery foliage which changes with the season. In spring, the new foliage is yellow-green, turning blue-green in summer and finally plum-purple in winter.

Uses Effective as specimen plants as well as accent plants amongst heathers. Good in mixed plantings of dwarf conifers in beds and borders. Also makes good container plants in very mild climate areas.

Planting Plant in spring. Allow each shrub a minimum 18in(45cm) spread at planting time with future provision for extra space, up to 2½ft(75cm).

Position Needs a mild climate plus a warm, sunny situation sheltered from strong winds.

Soil Best in an acid to neutral, moist well-drained soil of good average fertility. Use lime-free soil-based compost in containers.

Propagation Take semi-ripe heel or node cuttings during early autumn and root under cover.

Treatment Winter mulch during the first winter for frost protection and give container plants winter protection from frost and freezing wind throughout their lives.

Pruning Minimal cutting is required, shorten damaged or straggly growths in late spring or summer.

Problems Generally trouble free.

Thuja plicata 'Rogersii' (Western Red Cedar)

- Evergreen shrub
- Hardiness – H2
- Care – Easy to average

Description Height 16in(40cm) at 10 years, ultimately to 5ft(1.5m). Spread 12in(30cm) at 10 years, ultimately to 4ft(1.2m). This evergreen shrub makes a young dense compact bush of rounded shape, becoming more conical with age. The foliage is gold and bronze-green – colourings which persist all year round. Cones are not a feature.

Maturity Immediately effective from the day of planting.

Lifespan Given reasonable care and attention, has a useful garden life of 35 years.

Other varieties *T.p.* 'Cuprea', of similar habit to the above growing eventually to 3ft(90cm) high with a 2½ft(75cm) spread. The green foliage is tipped cream and gold, *T.p.* 'Stoneham Gold', broadly conical, growing ultimately to about 5ft(1.5m) in height. The foliage is bronze-green tipped with golden yellow – colourings are good year round.

Uses All these varieties make first-class rock garden plants, they are good in alpine raised beds and to include in mixed dwarf-conifer plantings in beds and borders. They make good accent plants midst heathers and are very good for container work.

Planting Preferably plant in spring although autumn is all right in mild climates. Allow each shrub a minimum 2ft(60cm) spread at planting time with the intention of clearing more space at a later date.

Position At its best in a mild climate. Needs a sunny, sheltered situation and protection from north and east winds.

Soil Flourishes in most well-drained moist soils of average fertility including those of an alkaline or heavy nature. Use soil-based potting compost in containers.

Propagation Ideally take semi-ripe cuttings in early autumn and root under cover before hardening off.

Pruning Little or no pruning needed apart from possible shortening of straggly or damaged growths in late spring or summer.

Problems Generally trouble free provided its cultural needs are met.

Index

INDEX

maintenance, 32–6, 45, 54–6, 69
mulching, 34–5, 55, 64, 67–9

noise screen, 16

parterre, 31
peat, 60, 62, 67
    bed, 27, 48
    pocket, rocky, 51, 52, 53
Pernettya, 9, 99, *100*
pests, 79–80
pH value, of soil, 38, 53
Picea, 109–10, 120–2
    Blue Spruce, *12*, *25*
    Mariana 'Nana', *65*, 122
Pieris japonica, 54
    'Little Heath', 9
    'Variegata', *100*
Pinus, *24*, 110–12, 122–4
    strobus 'Minuta', *36*
    sylvestris, *112*
planting, basin and mound, *63*
    incidental, 26, 31
    mixture, 48
    pits, 60, *61*
    pockets, 62
    position, 62
    seasons for, 22, 35, 37, 38, 46, 55
    spade, 62–3
    trowel, 63–4
plants, bracing, *83*
    buying, 46
    guying, *82*, 83
    preparation, 62
    supports, *64*
plunge beds, 34, 50, *52*, 53, *see also
    under* containers
poisonous plants, 14

pollution, 12, 37, 79
propagation, 36, 84–9
propagating case, *87*
pruning, 69, 72–7
    crown raising, 56, *81*
    crown thinning, 56, 83
    simple, 73
pygmy pinetum, 28, *29*

rainwater butt, *53*
raised beds, 50
red spider mite, 80
rhododendrons, dwarf, 54, 101
rock gardens, 18–19, 31, 34, *65*
    mound, 50, *51*, 60
roots, dryness, 62
    frost protection, 49–50
    pruning, 34
    structural damage by, 33–4

screening, 13–15, 31
seasonal garden, 27
seeds, 45, 87, 89
shaded garden, 28–9
shape of plants, 25–6
site, 7–8, 12, 22
    assessment, 36, 37
    clearance, 40–1
    drainage, 41–2
    levelling, 41
size of plants, 25–6
slopes and terracing, *39*, 40, 41
soakaway, rubble, 42
soils, 6–7, 11–12, 22, 37
    digging, 59–60
    drainage, 38, 41–2, 78
        subsoil water test, 38
        surface water penetration test, *39*

surface waterlogging, 42
    improvements, 58
    pH value, 38, 53
    texture, 38, 41
spring maintenance, 84–6
strip digging, *59*
style and plant choice, 22–3, 31
suckers, 35
summer maintenance, 69
sun, protection from, 78

Taxus baccata, *23*, 76, 112–13
    golden, *26*, 124
Thuja, 113–14
    blight, 35, 81
    occidentalis 'Rheingold', *19*, 124–5
    orientalis 'Aurea Nana', *125*, 126
    plicata 'Rogersii', *47*, 126
        'Zebrina', *11*
topdressing, 34, 55, 56, 69
topiary, 9, *22*, 29, *30*, 31, 69, 76–7
    archway, *76*
transplanting conifers, 42–4
tree heaths, 6, 13, 64
    pruning, *74*

undercutting, 42, *43*
underplanting, 31

Vaccinium, 54
    vitis idaea, 13, *27*, *101*

watering, 53, 55, 69–71
weed control, 68
wind effects, 37, 38, 55, 77
windowboxes, 35, 57, 66
windscreens, *15*, *78*
winter maintenance, 45